Asshole No More

"The two great wonders of the world
are not the Sphinx and the Pyramids;
they are
1) why assholes presume the
right to behave obnoxiously, and
2) why they are offended when
you catch them at it."

—St. Erculius
Early Christian Martyr
(or at least he thought he was)

This copy of
Asshole No More
is lovingly presented to:

_____

by :

_____

in the hope that
it will lead to
the road of recovery

Asshole No More

A Self-Help Guide
For Recovering Assholes—
And Their Victims

by Xavier Crement, M.D.

ENTHEA PRESS
Canal Winchester, Ohio

None of the names used in this book are the names of actual living people. Any resemblance between a person in this book and one in physical life is purely serendipitous and unintentional.

If you are offended by this book, there are three things you can do:

1) Ask the Iranian government to condemn the author and the book. (This will increase our sales tremendously.)

2) Organize a book burning party. This will attract the news media, and give us more free publicity.

3) Write a letter of protest to your congressman. Then he will know you are an asshole, too.

Table of Contents

For helping make this book possible, I thank—

Everyone who ever called me "asshole,"
But never tried to help me.

You know who you are.

This book is dedicated to *you*.

Introduction

Like almost everyone else, I have been dealing with assholes all of my life. For most of this time, however, I have been, like most of society, trapped in our age-old concepts of assholism. Failing to recognize it as a disease, I simply accepted it as a character flaw that could be modified or eliminated at will.

I have now come to understand the true nature of assholism. It is an addiction as bad as alcoholism, chemical dependency, or codependency. It afflicts major portions of the population—yet most assholes are not the least bit aware that they *are* assholes! This was certainly true in my own case—in my personal struggle to deal with being an asshole myself.

It is never easy to unveil one's own mistakes and flaws for all to see. For a long time, I hesitated to write this book, or even speak out on the topic that inspires it. I didn't want the whole world to know that I was an asshole! But finally my conscience, friends, and patients convinced me that the whole world already knew I was an asshole, and I could make a contribution by telling my story, so that others like me could understand assholism and embark on the road to recovery. It is therefore with the utmost humility that I have decided to share the story of my painful addiction to assholism—and the arduous path of recovery from its clutches.

At this point, I can look back with clarity and insight at the many years I was an asshole. I understand as only an asshole can the grief, pain, and struggle of the recovery process. It is not a process I would ever wish to go through again. But once you have become an asshole, you have no choice. Sooner or later, Life rears up before you and stops you in your tracks. It tells you, "You are an asshole." You will deny it, flail at it, damn it, scream at it, kick it, plead with it, try to ignore it, and curse it. But Life will not go away. Either you must humble yourself before it, or it will humble you.

It is therefore with great contrition and sorrow that I confess: *I was a flaming asshole for more than twenty years!* My friends and family suffered as much from my assholism as I did. In many cases, I simply drove them away. Even my patients suffered from my ingrained rudeness and outsized ego. I now recognize that all of this pain and suffering was avoidable—if I had just recognized the truth earlier and had begun my recovery at a younger age.

Take it from me—it is never too early or too late to recognize the telltale signs of being an asshole. Nor is it ever too early or too late to begin changing the destructive habits which have repelled your friends, sabotaged business and professional relationships, and brought years of unnecessary insult and offense to countless others.

In my case, I did not have the slightest clue that I was an asshole until I was nearly forty. Like most assholes, I took pride in the fact that I was a strong person who was always able to get what he wanted. I was still in high school when I first learned how to turn off my conscience and neutralize any sense or feeling of guilt. While I was in residency, I learned I could get what I wanted by intimidating people— in fact, I could usually make people do exactly what I wanted them to do. As I settled into my professional career, I further refined my skills of being cunning and aggressive.

It is important to understand that I thought all of these attributes were positive strengths. As part of my medical training, I took a barrage of psychological and psychiatric tests. They invariably rated me as a very strong person, reporting that I had "high self-esteem" and that I could take care of myself. I scored high in ego strength, I was well focused, I was self-determined, self-directing, and self-evaluating. In other words, no one could put me down, and if they tried, I could give them back as good as I got. I took pride in being able to "do it to them before they did it to me."

These attributes of character served me well. I became a successful and prosperous doctor specializing in proctology. I married a very attractive woman and we had two wonderful children. I was respected by my colleagues and held major positions in my hospital and local medical society. In my community, I was considered a professional with both affluence and influence. My life seemed charmed. I was content with life and content with myself.

But all was not well in the empire of Dr. X. Crement. At times, I had the eerie feeling that my

9

colleagues had more fear than respect for me—but I figured it didn't make much difference, so long as it was some shade of awe. Some of my colleagues would seem to break off conversations and quickly walk away as I approached them at the hospital, and certain friends seemed to have a growing number of excuses for not being able to get together with me. At meetings, some people would stare at the floor or the ceiling with a blank expression, fidgeting while I talked. Afterwards, it was as though they had not heard a word I had said. But I figured that was their problem. They were probably worried about personal difficulties.

One time, my wife gave a surprise birthday party for me, but the biggest surprise was that only six people showed up, and three of them were my wife and kids. But I just assumed that my friends were becoming jealous of my brilliant success. I thought it was unfortunate that they would alienate themselves from me over something so petty as their own inferiority and inadequacy, but I just chalked it up to human nature. Being a thoughtful, sensitive person—or so I believed—I regarded these social lapses and snubs with compassion and forgiveness.

Then one day, my self-delusion began to unravel. After arguing with me for hours, my only son announced that he was not going to enter college; he was determined to enlist in the Navy. My only son was going to defy me! I couldn't believe it! No one had dared defy me in at least twenty years, and the last one who had had long since regretted it.

I wanted my son to be a successful professional just like myself, but he was obstinate. This solidified

10

my resolve as well, and I forbad him to join the Navy. He told me to perform an operation which would not be all that difficult for a proctologist, although distinctly undesirable, and stormed out of the house. He told my wife that he was determined to get as far away from me as possible, and he was right. He signed up for astronaut training.

I was deeply confused and hurt by the acts of my only son. In my anguish, I asked my wife and my daughter what they thought about this turn of events. I was looking for them to validate that I was a good father, and that it was my son who was acting foolishly.

"I love that boy," I said tearfully. "What did I do to deserve such rebellion?"

I was certainly not prepared for the response I received. My daughter spoke first. "The only person you've ever loved," she said smoothly, "is yourself."

I was stunned. Finally, I turned to my wife as my last hope for support.

"She's right," my wife confirmed. "In fact, our marriage and home life has been dead for at least five years. I want you out of the house tonight."

I could not believe what was happening to me. Within just a few hours, my personal world had come tumbling down.

I spent a number of days reviewing this turn of events. In my heart, I knew I was right—as I often had been over the years, despite ferocious opposition. Someone had been alienating my loved ones and had turned them against me. When I found out who it was, I resolved to smash his face in.

Many times before, I had had to face those who

were united in opposing my beliefs and behavior. Only the pure force of will had helped me preserve my dignity and self-respect. Finally, I decided that this situation was no different than the others. Winning back my family would be my greatest triumph of all. But everything I did to win them back failed. They would not see me. They would not speak to me. We became more and more estranged. In desperation, I began to realize that *I needed outside help!*

So I consulted with a psychiatric colleague of mine. I explained what had been happening and asked him what was wrong. What had come over my family? Were they sick? I pleaded with him to tell me the unvarnished truth; I was a strong man and could handle it, whatever it was.

My friend paused, then looked directly at me. "They are not sick; they're normal."

It took awhile for the implication to sink in. It was almost too much for me to handle.

"Y-y-you mean, I'm the one who's sick?"

"No, you're not sick, either. You're just an asshole."

I was shocked and angered by this flippant response. "I didn't come here to be insulted! If you can't take my problems seriously, I'm leaving!" So I left.

The next six months were as close to hell on earth, or at least hell in a proctologist's office, as you can imagine. I felt sorry for myself and saw myself as the victim of unknown forces—misunderstood and neglected by those I loved and mistreated by those I had consulted for professional help. I would be angry one day and sorrowful the next—but I was never happy or even contented. I did not sleep well. I was on edge all the time. I saw every interruption, delay, or complication as a mysterious vendetta against me. I do not know how the nurses on my staff—or my patients, for that matter—put up with me during that time. I was a monster.

Finally, one evening—alone—I realized that I had lost control of my life. I then also realized that I had never actually had control of my life—I had just arrogantly assumed that I did. Somehow, this revelation comforted me, and I slept better that night than I had in six months.

The next day, while performing a proctoscopic examination, the rest of the pieces of the puzzle suddenly came together. Staring at my patient's rear end, I suddenly realized that I was confronting the naked truth about myself.

I *was* an asshole!

My psychiatric colleague had not been insulting me after all; he had been trying to help me! I called him immediately, apologized for my rude behavior, and asked to see him again.

Since he had just had a cancellation, I was able to see him that afternoon.

"You're right," I told him breathlessly as soon as I sat down. "I am an asshole."

He yawned. "Actually, everyone knows it."

"How are you going to treat it?"

"Treat what?"

"My being an asshole."

"It's not a disease," my colleague said, "it's just a condition. So there is no treatment."

"What do you mean, there is no treatment?"

"Look. Lot's of people are assholes. Either you

are or you are not. It's like being left-handed. It can't be treated."

I was shocked. "What good is psychiatry if it cannot cure someone of being an asshole?"

"Look. It's not a disease; it's a figure of speech. Proctology can't cure people who have their heads wedged up their asses, and psychiatry can't cure you of being an asshole. Hell, if it could, do you think so many psychiatrists would still be assholes?"

It was at that moment that I realized that I was on my own. Somehow, deep in my being, I knew that he was wrong. Assholism is not a character disorder. It is a disease—an addiction to crude and rude behavior that leaves us helpless to recognize our own denial of our personal, ingrained arrogance, bigotry, and aggressiveness.

I therefore began an intensive program of introspection, healing, and growth that has lasted for several years. I have proved what my colleague thought was impossible—*assholes can recover!* As incredible as this may seem to the unredeemed asshole, all it takes is the rediscovery of our own basic humanity.

I wish I had started the process of recovery sooner, before I had done so much damage to others. But I have been able to repair much of the injury. My wife has come back to me, and we are enjoying a second honeymoon. My daughter has forgiven me, and she is a junior in college. My son has made a career of being a Navy pilot, and is in the process of teaching me how to fly.

I have given up the practice of proctology, but I am still in the business of seeing assholes. I have become a psychiatrist who specializes in helping assholes identify their problem and embark on the road to recovery. There has not been much support from traditional branches of psychiatry for this pioneering effort, but I have enjoyed a huge surge in business, as my basic message has spread throughout the country: "At last, there is hope for assholes!" I have become a popular speaker on the lecture circuit, and network with other therapists dealing with addictive problems, too.

Asshole No More is more than just my personal story of recovery, however. It is a spark of hope for every addict of assholism. It is a declaration of liberation. No one ever again needs to feel ashamed to be an asshole. It is a legitimate illness that can be treated by legitimate means. There isn't an asshole alive who cannot follow the same road to recovery that I have—the road that I have now helped thousands of people successfully follow.

There is only one requirement—the courage to stop being an asshole. This is often the most elusive ingredient in the whole formula. Calvin Stobbs, a friend of mine who runs a mental health clinic, likes to tell a story that drives home this point.

There once was a woman who went to find the meaning of life in the mountains of the Himalayas. After years of searching, she came across a man in a cave. "Ah-ha!" she thought, "A guru meditating in a cave." She spoke to the man. "Will you show me the way to enlightenment?" The man said nothing.

So the woman sat down and began tuning in to her innermost self. At the end of the day, she got up to go. "Have I made any progress?" she asked. The man said nothing.

The next day she returned at the crack of dawn

and began meditating again. When the sun was setting, she rose again to go. Once more, she asked, "Have I made any progress?" The man said nothing.

This pattern went on for weeks and then months. Finally, she got fed up with waiting. At sunset that day, she stood up and began yelling and screaming at the old man:

"You are a fraud! I have been sitting here day after day, waiting for enlightenment, and nothing has happened. I've just wasted six months of my life and have nothing to show for it! How dare you call yourself a guru!" And she threw her knapsack, which weighed almost forty pounds, at the old man sitting in the cave.

Dazed by the blow, the man nonetheless was able to get up on his feet. Standing there, he spoke at last. "I am not a guru, and I do not deserve these accusations. If you assumed I was a guru, that is your own mistake, not mine."

The woman was not to be appeased. "Well, if you are not a guru," she said, "then who the hell are you and what are you doing in this cave?"

The man pulled himself up proudly. "I am a leper," he said, "and I am here in this cave as an exile from my community."

That's what this book is all about: learning what it means to wake up and realize that you are an asshole.

I woke up. You can, too.

Asshole No More:

Part One: What's An Asshole And Why Would Anyone Become One?

1
Fred's Story

All my best friends told me I would love him, and I did. But no one ever told me he was an asshole. Some friends!
—Winifred, dumped by an asshole

This is Fred's story. I'll let him tell it.

* * *

I slumped in my chair at my desk in the office, too tired to face the rest of the day. It was only 9:15 in the morning, but the day was already turning into a disaster. I was on the verge of a complete breakdown. It hadn't taken much to whip me into such a state.

I had felt okay when I awoke. But the tide began to turn as soon as I pulled into my favorite eatery for breakfast. Every morning, I order exactly the same thing: a three-minute egg, bacon, toast, juice, and coffee. And they know that when I order a three-minute egg, I want it cooked exactly three minutes. It was ready as usual for me, but the egg was overdone. They had let it cook at least thirty seconds too long! I couldn't understand why they would deliberately overcook my egg! I called Meg—the waitress—over to my table and pointed out that the egg was overdone. She gave me a dirty look, as though to say, "Here we go again," and then said in a huffy tone of voice: "So we'll put it back in the pot and uncook it. How underdone would you like your egg?"

I told her if she was going to bark at me, she could forget a tip for today. Five minutes later, after having had to ask her three times to refill my coffee cup, she dumped the whole pot in my lap! She said it was an accident, but I wasn't born yesterday.

If breakfast wasn't bad enough, the rest of the trip to work was worse. A cop stopped me for going 50 in a 35 mile-an-hour zone, then gave me a second ticket because I wasn't wearing my seat belt. By this time, I was plenty steamed, so I asked him why he wasn't spending his time arresting the asshole that nearly ran me off the road two miles back, instead of me. He added a charge of resisting arrest on top of the other two. Now I will need a small loan just to keep on driving.

When I arrived at work, I pulled into my parking spot as usual. When I got out, I stepped right into a huge pile of horse shit. Somebody must be trying to get even with me, but I haven't had time to figure out who it might be. There are a lot of candidates.

And that wasn't the last of it. On the way up to my office—it's on the top floor—the elevator jammed, trapping me between the third and fourth floors. It didn't take all that long to get the elevator running again, but I distinctly heard someone on the fourth floor say, "It's Fred who's stuck. Can't we just leave him there all day?" I must make a note to sack the maintenance crew later on, for letting the elevator get jammed.

I used to thrive on adversity like this, but now it just wears me down. I hate to lose—and I almost never did earlier in my life. But now I seem to be on the losing end a lot. It's making me depressed and fatigued. I'm not sure I still have the *cojones* to do what has to be done.

I guess it's the winning/losing thing. I have always had to be the winner. When I was a kid, I excelled in all of the usual sports and games. Sometimes I had to cheat to win, but that was part of the fun. I loved to pick arguments with my brothers just so I could win them. My greatest moments of triumph came when I was able to outwit my parents and get them to do exactly what I wanted.

In high school, I went out for the debate team as well as athletics. I learned how to use words to intimidate my opponents and turn ideas inside out so that no one could recognize them anymore. In everything I did, I tried to find the trick that would give me an advantage and enable me to win. I thrived on winning. It was the thrill that I lived for.

During adolescence, the scope of my winning expanded to include girls. I became intoxicated by the thrill of conquest. Sexy girls, shapely girls, tall girls, short girls—the more elusive the girl was, the more I wanted to conquer her. And then I would move on to my next target.

Thinking back on it, I guess the reason why I hated to lose was because of the way my older brothers treated me. They made fun of me because I was younger and smaller, so I always tried to exceed my limits. Nothing was sweeter than being able to outdo my brothers. Of course, as I got older and bigger, this began to happen more and more often.

I had promised myself, when I was small and helpless, to get even—and I did!

I think my old man got a kick out of it, too, whenever I was able to outdo my brothers, or anyone older than me. More than once I overheard him mumble, in a voice that was barely audible, "One of these days, the little shit is going to be a big pile of shit, just like his old man."

I went to law school, graduated with honors, and was asked to join a large law firm. Twenty years later, I am now a full partner making six figures every year, while my brothers are only partners in the family business that my father started.

Being a winner has not always been easy. I knew I was entering a dog-eat-dog world of fierce competition and back-stabbing—there's enough of that in law school, let alone the real world. I also knew that I could not dare give anyone else even the slightest break—and I never did. Winning in life depends on learning all of the tricks and in taking advantage of every opening that appears. I trained myself to out-dazzle, outdance, and outbullshit everyone!

I dressed for success.

I worked out regularly, to keep myself lean and mean—especially mean.

I took classes in effective communications—in how to put people at ease so that you can manipulate them more readily.

I learned to lie, cheat, and dissemble and yet appear to be the most forthright and honest person around. I learned when to kick ass—and when to kiss it. If I hadn't been an attorney, I think I would have made a good used car salesman.

But I am an attorney, and a damn good one. I soon came to enjoy the power I wielded. I enjoyed it even more when I was able to bend the law to serve my own purposes—the more devious, the better. Any yo-yo can use the law for legitimate purposes, but it takes a skilled craftsman to bend it consistently to promote self-serving and sometimes even illegal purposes.

Most of all, I enjoy intimidating all those wimps out there—the sweet, gentle, honest types that were born to lose. I believe my biggest contribution to life is to teach these pathetic creatures what it means to be strong and bold—a winner!

I have never married, but I don't regret it for a minute. I can have companionship any time I want it, and it's cheaper than buying a house and supporting a wife and kids. I never let a woman get to know me well enough to start nagging me!

I spend most of my time at work. I know I am a winner there, because an awful lot of my clients, who walked into the hall of justice guilty as hell, walked out as free men and women. Some of them I have successfully defended seven or eight times.

I love to work in front of a jury. There's the ultimate challenge the law provides—to convince eight people that your client is as innocent as a baby's butt, even though he's got the cash he stole in his back pocket.

It's not just me, though—I expect my staff to be winners, too. I keep them on their toes. They know I do not tolerate mistakes. Occasionally, one of them will try to cover up a mistake they've made by suggesting that I made it impossible for them to do anything else. But I do not let any of them blame me for their failings! The one thing I will not tolerate is a smart ass, either working for me or as a client. I am the boss. No one has the right to tell me what to do or criticize my performance.

But I am getting tired of the hassles I get from my staff. Whatever happened to loyalty? I have had to replace the whole office staff several times in the last three years. You just can't find good secretaries and typists anymore. It's gotten to the point where I don't even know the names of the people I'm blaming.

I was able to handle the turnover okay, but recently my partners have begun to bug me about low morale. As if it's *my* fault for wanting the office to run smoothly and efficiently! I'll have to go along with them, though; I don't want the other partners to start prying into my activities too deeply, lest they discover the sizeable sums I have "borrowed" from the partnership account.

And it's not just the staff and my partners giving me flak! In the last month alone, three of my clients have sued me for malpractice. I'll admit I lost their cases, but I just wasn't able to get through to the juries. They were too stupid to be misled by my clever tricks. Some cases go like that.

I'll handle these suits the way I have always handled dissatisfied clients; by the time I am done with them, they'll wish they had never heard of malpractice. But I don't understand why they can't learn to lose gracefully—after all, they've been losers all their lives. Does that give them the right to accuse me of selling them out to the other side? I would never do a thing like that—unless the other side had been willing to pay a whole lot more than they offered.

You can understand why I am tired of it all. I am beginning to think there is a cost to winning at any cost—and I may not be willing to pay it any longer.

* * *

I met Fred at this point. He was about to learn three fundamental truths:

1. He was not really a winner—he was just an asshole. Assholism is an illness that takes over and makes one behave in very antisocial ways. He was not actually tired of life—just tired of being an asshole and getting dumped on by everyone else in retribution.

2. Once a person becomes an asshole, the disease takes on a life of its own and feeds itself. It's like catching a case of herpes—it leads to unpleasant complications. Once you realize you can win by cheating or bullying people, you become caught in a cycle that is hard to break.

3. If you want to get rid of assholism, you have to do something about it yourself. It doesn't matter that other people are nasty and incompetent and out to get you. It doesn't even matter that most other people are also assholes. If you are an asshole, your only real enemy is yourself. *Only you can wipe out assholism!*

Fred was the kind of asshole who is almost incurable—a man with a bulletproof ego. When I first told him he was an asshole, his reply was:

"So's your sister."

"Yes, that's absolutely true," I replied, "although I didn't realize you knew her."

"I meant that as an insult," Fred said.

"Why?" I asked.

"Because you're as much an asshole as I am."

"And that's why I am able to help you," I said.

Later on, Fred told me that the only reason he decided to start on the road to recovery was because I had confused him more than he had ever been confused before. This illustrates an important point. The actual steps of recovery will probably vary from asshole to asshole. This is not a precise science. Each asshole must determine the nature of the healing process for himself or herself. But always, the first step is to admit that you are an asshole, confess that you have hurt others, and then resolve to become a decent human being—a DHB.

Once this first step has been taken, then it becomes possible to take the other steps of recovery:

• Understanding the complete emptiness of character and humanity that forms the core of your assholism. Some recovering assholes refer to this emptiness as "the abyss." Others just call it the hole.

• Learning that it is possible to fill this abyss with qualities and types of behavior that will actually attract other people and inspire them to be your friends, instead of leaving piles of horseshit for you to step in.

• Discovering that you can indeed make a difference in this thing we call Life. In fact, every asshole who reforms himself or herself improves the quality of life on earth far more than any of us can imagine.

These changes are not easy ones to make, because they will require a complete turnabout in your thinking and attitudes as a human being. You will be shocked to discover what your friends and family really think about you. You may even become depressed, and start to feel shame and guilt for the first time. These can be painful experiences for the recovering asshole. But hang in there—the payoff is worth it.

I am pleased to report that Fred's story has a happy ending. He finally discovered that there are more losers in the world than winners, and if he wanted to be liked, he had to get along with them, too. He has married Meg, sold his BMW to the cop who arrested him, and recently gave large raises to everyone in his office, in appreciation for the grief and insults they had suffered at his hands. He then resigned from his practice and joined the Peace Corps in Afghanistan. His farewell party was the largest send-off in the history of his law firm.

2
Other Stories

> When I say I was an asshole, I don't mean a casual asshole. I was an asshole with a capital A. I wasn't content to just be obnoxious. I was a tyrant. I was only happy if I was in the process of destroying the self-respect and happiness of everyone around me.
> —Priscilla, a recovering asshole

You may have recognized something of your own character in the story about Fred in the last chapter. His kind of story is one that I hear often. But the arrogant, pushy, ambitious dickhead is not the only kind of asshole that exists. There are many other varieties of assholes that must be considered as well.

Some of these are illustrated in the following tales.

* * *

Alexis is tall, attractive, and blond. Now in her late thirties, she thinks of herself as a success in her career but a failure in her personal relationships. In this regard, she is like many other assholes: she doesn't know very much about herself.

Alexis has always been popular with the boys— at least those who could afford the steep prices she exacted for her favors. A date with Alexis could easily be rewarding, but it was not like taking candy from a baby. It was more like selling your soul to the devil.

Nonetheless, she always was able to find men who were willing to pay the price. They bought her the best clothing and jewels; they helped her with loans she never had to repay. She always had a hot car to drive and an expensive apartment to live in, even though she was fond of making the statement: "I don't make payments for anything." To her, that was the reason why men existed: to open the door for her, to accent her natural beauty as they stood next to her, and to pay her bills.

Alexis found her niche in an advertising agency, where adroit maneuvering and the skillful use of other people's ideas helped her advance quickly up the agency's ladder. Alexis was smooth, almost cat-like on the job. She never engaged in open combat, but always managed to outwit everyone around her. She knew when to withhold information and hide important memos, thereby making her colleagues look like thumbsucking fools. She was a master at taking credit for triumphs she had nothing to do with, and dodging blame for disasters worse than the Hindenberg.

She used her personal charm and seductiveness to bring many new clients into the agency—and to encourage existing clients to request that they put her in charge of their account. She was the number one account executive in her agency, and she enjoyed the power and perks of her position. Alexis was proud of the fact that so many people envied her. She also knew that if she ever had to work for a living, she would be in big trouble, but what the heck—she was in advertising!

Still, she was uneasy about her personal life. Oh, it was a lot of fun during her twenties and most of the way through her thirties. But as she grew older, something within began to nag her. Was she successful—or just a whore?

She was skillful enough to avoid confronting this dilemma, of course, but it seeped up into her thinking in camouflaged ways, anyway. She became more and more dissatisfied with the men who went out with her. If they were rich enough for her, they were either too old or too fat. If they were handsome and young enough for her, they were either poor or lacked power. If they adored her, she knew they were too dumb to see the real her—the inner phoniness behind all that outer phoniness. If they pushed her around and insisted on being in charge, she quickly lost interest in them. It was all right for a man to take charge in bed, but if it carried over into the rest of their relationship, she was unable to accept it.

But the growing uneasiness about men was only half of the story. For the truth was that Alexis had no friends. She had only contempt for her co-workers, and they returned the favor with hostility. She fought continuously with her neighbors—about where she could park her car (one common suggestion was anatomically impossible), how loud she could play her stereo system, and her disarming habit of walking down the hall of her apartment building half-naked. Her male neighbors did not seem to mind this particular habit, but their wives became venomous whenever the subject arose.

She couldn't even turn to her mother for advice and comfort, because she hadn't spoken to her for years—not since the time her mother had scolded her for breaking curfew and grounded her for a week. She refused to accept her phone calls, and returned all her letters unopened.

Poor Alexis. She was talented, rich, and successful, but she was unhappy. Was she a victim of other people's rudeness and envy?

Or was she just an asshole?

When Alexis came to me for counseling, I discovered that her mother had been a tyrannical parent, frequently criticizing her and rarely complimenting her for her successes. Her mother had been jealous of her daughter's talent and beauty, and had tried to sabotage her happiness by inducing guilt and self-doubt.

The diagnosis was easy. "Your mother," I told Alexis, "is an asshole."

"You're charging me $100 an hour to tell me what I already know?" she asked. She was starting to become hostile, but I checked her by raising my finger. Perhaps she innately realized I used to be a proctologist; in any event, she let me continue.

"And you are the adult child of an asshole parent," I continued.

"Oh," she said. "Well, that makes sense." I could tell she was relieved to have someone else to blame. "You have walled yourself off from her tyranny," I added, "but at the price of also walling yourself off from all meaningful human contact."

"What does that mean?" she asked.

"It means you have become an asshole, too."

With counseling and the help of a support group, Alexis has been able to accept her addiction to assholism and to recognize how this had driven her to cheat, lie, and manipulate others in order to stay on top of her life. I took a direct interest in helping her revise her attitudes toward sex, and must say that the therapy has been a rousing success.

Today, she lives in Pittsburgh where she works as a sales clerk at a K-Mart. She is happily married to an unemployed steel worker. They have one lovely child, with another on the way.

* * *

Hubert came to me as a child of nine. His parents referred to him as "Damien." At school, they labeled him "emotionally disadvantaged." Four therapists had given up on him, and two of them had abandoned psychotherapy to go into less stressful work—lion taming and undercover narcotics investigation. Most people called him a spoiled brat. In actual fact, he was an asshole.

Hubert's story illustrates very plainly that not all assholes are the product of a rotten childhood. That explanation worked in the case of Alexis, but it won't fly here. Hubert did not have a rotten childhood—he *was* a rotten child!

Hubert's basic problem was that he hated to see anyone else having fun. If a group of girls was quietly having a tea party, Hubert was incapable of letting them be. He was apt to go running over to them, like a kamikaze pilot, and divebomb the tea party, sending plates and tea and little girls flying in all directions.

This is the kind of kid who would dump dog turds in a public swimming pool, so that it had to be closed down and everyone sent home.

He did have his strengths, though. Here is one kid who would never cheat in order to pass an exam. He would just show up on the front step of his teacher's home with a loaded rifle and scare the hell out of her.

Hubert's case was a difficult one, largely due to his commitment to malice. When I first told him that he was an asshole, he smiled broadly and said that I was the first adult who had ever said anything nice about him. I knew at that moment that we were in deep doo doo with this one.

I am not without resourcefulness, however. I relied on my former days as an asshole and a proctologist to handle the lad.

"Then let's show you what it feels like to be an asshole," I said. Grabbing him from behind, I pulled down his pants and gave him a three-finger rectal examination. From that moment on, I have enjoyed complete cooperation from young Hubert, and I am happy to report that he will be getting his Eagle badge in Boy Scouts next month.

* * *

Walter is a minister. He was ordained fourteen years ago and has held appointments in twelve churches in that time. He is an ardent student of the Bible and has a special interest in counseling. He considers himself an expert on sin, mental illness, and spiritual martyrdom. In fact, he often thinks of himself as the quintessential martyr, devoting himself selflessly to his work and service.

In his sermons, Walter tells it straight. We have a duty to be perfect in God's eyes, Walter will say, and he who falls short of perfection *falls all the way.* "If God knows when a sparrow falls," Walter is fond of saying, "then you had better believe that He knows when you or I fall. And He doesn't forget."

At times, Walter's style in the pulpit becomes bellicose, almost belligerent. A sane person might wonder if Walter was starting to come unglued. On more than one occasion, in fact, the church board has called Walter to task for this belligerence, but he has always been prepared for the attack, and has fended off the criticisms with pious poses and phrases. He reminds the board that God's servants have many enemies, and a church board must never let itself be used by those who would undo the work of the Lord.

One Sunday, however, Walter chose to preach on the subject of adultery. In his usual style, he came down hard on the sin, ranting and raving about how God held it as a great abomination. He told the congregation that hell was lined with those who had committed adultery, and held out little hope and even less mercy for those who had erred in this way.

The very next Sunday, just as Walter was beginning his pastoral prayer, one of the men in the congregation stood up and began waving a gun in the air. "You had better make this prayer a good one," the gentleman said, "because it may well be your last one. And be sure to ask the Lord to forgive you for adultery and fornication, because if you don't stay away from my wife and daughters, I'm going to personally escort you to the gates of hell."

Walter handled the unpleasant situation with great poise and piety. He told the congregation that the gentleman's accusations were false, but that he, Walter, could forgive him for his outrageous behavior. Many people in the church wept openly, moved by his pious, almost saintly tolerance.

But Walter's days were numbered. The very next day, an ad hoc committee of cuckolded husbands and irate fathers sent a letter to the presiding bishop, asking that Walter be removed from their church and defrocked as a minister. The bishop called for a private hearing. Walter continued to deny the accusations, but his accusers had come well prepared. They had explicit color photographs of Walter in action, as well as tape recordings of tearful spouses and daughters. Confronted with the evidence, Walter was still unrepentant. He said it was just his way of fufilling the commandment to love your neighbor. A minister must toil day and night—and sometimes beneath the sheets as well.

Walter was shipped off to his thirteenth church, but the bishop kept the color photographs—just in case.

The final blow came when his wife announced she was taking the children, returning to the home of her parents, and accepting a job with a foundation promoting world atheism. Walter was stunned. He had always assumed that the bishop would protect him and his wife would stand by him, no matter what. He searched and searched for a rationalization or pious phrase to rescue him, but there were none. He was surrounded by enemies—and no one was there to save him. It must be the work of the devil, he concluded.

But was it the devil? Or was Walter just an asshole?

It was the bishop who put Walter in touch with me. I helped him see through the veneer of his piety and realize that he was not the kind, considerate, compassionate, and moral person he thought he had been. He was just a pious asshole.

This was not an easy task, for Walter had to confront the fact that he had raised self-deception to an art form. He had convinced himself that everything he had done was not only honorable, but something of a self-sacrifice. He had seen his alliances with the ladies of the church, for instance, as a way of healing their loneliness and helping them cope with insensitive husbands.

Finally, though, he began to realize that he was not God's greatest gift to womanhood—or anyone. He saw how much he had hurt people and abused his responsibilities. I shall never forget the day he looked up at me and beamed, "Boy, have I been an asshole!" It's moments like these that make my work as a psychiatrist worthwhile.

After many months of counseling and therapy, Walter consented to the request of his wife for a divorce. He also left the church. His hardest lesson was learning that other people were not put on earth to amuse and serve him. He therefore has had to learn a whole new way of behaving.

Walter is now working as a camel driver in Iran,

employed by Shiite Moslem holy men. He claims he has found God again—the real God. "If God can forgive militant bomb throwers like these Shiites and assholes like me, He must be the greatest power in the universe!" Walter says. If you ask Walter now for guidance or help, he cheerfully replies: "Never take advice from an asshole!"

The evening desert breezes seem to whisper back in a soft murmur: "That's right."

* * *

From these few stories, we can learn several things about assholism. It can strike the rich and the poor, men and women, and the young or the old alike. Being intelligent is no safeguard against assholism, but neither is stupidity. Assholism is a disease that can strike anywhere, anytime, without warning.

As a rabbi who has seen more than his share of assholes for one lifetime recently remarked, "Anyone can be rude, given the right circumstances. Once the occasion has passed, an ordinary person will retreat into embarrassment and contrition. An asshole will go looking for another opportunity."

I chose these stories because they reflect the diversity of ways that assholes behave. No one case of assholism is ever typical, however. People are complex. Assholism is complex. The road to recovery from assholism is likewise complex. It may well take more than a single book to describe it completely. I'll have to see how well this one sells before I make that decision, though.

37

There are at least 100 million assholes in this country alone. Each case is unique. I could write a lot of books before running out of things to say, couldn't I?

Yet there are certain characteristics that can be ascribed to the common asshole:

- Blind selfishness.
- Unrestrained obnoxiousness.
- Arrogant righteousness.
- An asbestos-proof conscience (it won't even burn in hell).
- Contempt for authority.
- The total rejection of basic human decency.
- The merciless exploitation of the innocent.

We will examine these characteristics and others in a couple of chapters. Don't worry about them at this point. As your therapist will probably tell you, sooner or later, "It's okay to feel overwhelmed."

ACTIVITY

1. Did any of these case histories remind you of someone—perhaps the person you first see in the mirror each morning? What specifics made you think of yourself? What obnoxious behavior reminded you of things you have done to others?

2. You may find it helpful to purchase *a very large* notebook to set down these observations, as well as other insights that come to you, as you continue reading this book.

3
Defining Assholism

> The greatest mystery of the world
> is not why God created life; it is
> why He named the asshole after
> such rude and obnoxious people.
> —Graffiti found on the wall of the
> men's room in an old Boston church.

So far, I have been using the labels *asshole* and *assholism* without defining them clearly. Yet the terms themselves are rather loose, defying precise definition. Asshole behavior in one situation may be acceptable social conduct in another. I for one would never dream of being defended in court by any kind of lawyer but an asshole. So no one simple definition is apt to do justice to the amazing complexity of assholism.

Still, this is not an insurmountable problem. Most people would agree: "I may not be able to define what an asshole is, but I sure know one when I see one." And this is true. Almost everyone would agree that an asshole is a person who behaves obnoxiously and rudely by choice, delighting in the chaos it produces and the annoyance it causes others.

39

There will always be nitpickers who will protest that this kind of definition is too loose and casual to be used by professional therapists. My answer to that is: let them pick their own nits!

Others object that the word *asshole* is a low-life slang word that is used only to condemn and ridicule. It can therefore have no proper use in a clinical setting, lest we hurt some poor asshole's feelings. These folks obviously don't know much about assholism—they are overlooking the fact that assholes have no feelings. An asshole's feelings cannot be hurt until he begins the road to recovery.

Some people complain that the term *assholism* is too subjective—that assholes exist only in the eye of the beholder. Personally, as a former proctologist, I believe this particular notion is going way too far.

I feel I must therefore make a bold statement. There is enormous therapeutic value in retaining the term *asshole*. For one thing, it has a rich depth of association to it that ordinary clinical terms lack—terms such as paranoid, deviate behavior, and so on. Yes, *asshole* is a highly prejudiced term. But assholism is not a prissy disease. It is true that ordinary people are offended to be called assholes. But ordinary people are not assholes. Assholes are rude, obnoxious, and intimidating—and proud of it. They need a label that makes everyone laugh at them.

Many people drink, but no one wants to be called an alcoholic. That is why the first step in the Twelve Step program is to admit that you are an alcoholic. It is also why it is paramount for the asshole to begin his path to recovery by saying: "I am an asshole." The statement "I am a rude dude" just doesn't carry the same impact.

What these naysayers are failing to realize is that assholism is, in fact, a disease. It is not just the simple lack of politeness. It is not even a habitual tendency to rebel. These are character flaws. Assholism is an *addiction* to power, a contempt for authority, a never-ending craving for approval, and the lust for complete control of others. It ravages the inner stability of its victims, leaving them helpless to act like decent human beings—until they confess, "I am an asshole."

These beliefs of mine have been confirmed by people the world over.

"Don't tell me there aren't any assholes in the world," said one angry housewife who heard me speak. "I've had to live with four of them—my husband and three of my kids. Anyone who thinks there aren't any assholes must be an asshole."

"I can spot an asshole a mile away," says a waitress at a MacDonald's in Sacramento. "They're smart asses—the kind of person who thinks a quarter pounder is a prophylactic."

"I had no idea how many other people were assholes, too, until I started recovery," says a recovering asshole. "I soon realized that all my friends were assholes, too. But when I suggested they come to a recovery meeting with me, they just laughed an asshole laugh."

"I lost my job and my family because I was an asshole," says another recovering asshole. "I tried to control the whole world, but I couldn't even control myself. I was a power junkie gone berserk. It was pathetic."

41

Some therapists have gone so far as to claim that everyone is an asshole, once you get to know them. For them, it's probably true. But otherwise, this theory only applies to evangelists and lawyers.

A Brief History of Assholism

There have always been assholes. Now, there are more assholes than ever. This is all anyone needs to know about the history of assholism.

The Real Poop on Assholes

The epidemiology of assholism indicates that there are many "high risk groups" for assholes (see chart on next page). A large number can be found in positions of authority which require no talent—for example, low-level bureaucrats, preachers, social workers, and any I'm-out-to-save-the-world-even-if-I-have-to-kill-you types. People who wear "Thank you for not smoking" buttons and organize local recycling programs in their communities are almost sure to be assholes.

The law enforcement profession produces an unusually high ratio of assholes. But the highest percentage is to be found in agents of the Internal Revenue Service, who act as though their motto is: "Asshole is our middle name."

The statistical findings of these various studies will undoubtedly permit many asshole students to earn doctoral degrees in psychology for generations to come. For a more definitive study of assholes,

HIGH RISK GROUPS OF ASSHOLES

1. Internal Revenue Service agents.
2. Traffic cops.
3. Bureaucrats.
4. Lawyers.
5. Anyone who wants to save whales.
6. People who *enjoy* living in New York City.
7. Insurance adjustors.
8. Anyone who drives as if he owns the road.
9. People who say, "Have a nice day."
10. Evangelists.
11. Congressmen.
12. Psychiatrists and psychologists.
13. Newspaper and magazine critics.
14. People who ditch in line.
15. Bill collectors.
16. Anyone who's offended by split infinitives.
17. Marxist college professors.
18. The Iranian government.
19. Women at a sale.
20. Anyone with a "cause."
21. People who write books about assholes.
22. People who play car stereos on full volume.
23. Union negotiators.
24. Women who don't shave their legs.
25. Anyone doing unsolicited telephone sales.
26. Zoning commissions.
27. People who argue while dining in public.
28. Parents of kids who run wild in public places.
29. Dictators whose first name is "Saddam."
30. Anyone who takes this book seriously.

examine *Assholes Among Us,* by H.M. Rhoid, Ph.D. Dr. Rhoid brilliantly builds proof for his thesis that assholes are people who are drawn to assume positions of power. He finds no evidence that any politician, evangelist, or therapist is inherently an asshole—it is their assholism that drives them to go into professions in which they can dominate others and lord it over them with petty power.

Like many diseases, assholism can be inherited. Many of today's assholes are simply the adult children of asshole parents. Some children of assholes are so repulsed by their parents' example that they shun all traits of assholism as they mature. But most are infected by the asshole virus, and end up being a rude chip off of a crude shoulder.

One of the easiest ways to define assholes is to study their dominant characteristics. Most assholes can be spotted by their aggressive behavior and intimidating mannerisms. If they can't get their way by pushing and shoving others out of it, then they will cheat—or change the rules to suit their needs. In emergency situations, they may even resort to screaming, yelling, foot stomping, and holding their breath. Nikita Khrushchev, when he pounded the desk at the U.N. with his shoe and proclaimed that he would bury the West, was demonstrating world-class assholism in action.

When assholes are caught being assholes, they tend to deny everything and quickly turn the tables, criticizing the person who blew the whistle on them for being so rude as to notice their own dishonesty. If cornered, the asshole will spout and fume and complain that he has been set up or framed, and demand exoneration.

As is the case with all addictions, denial is a special problem of the asshole. Assholes deny the need to be responsible—or even consistent. They deny that they have any problems or faults. Worst of all, they deny that they even have an obligation to act as decent human beings.

This is not to say that they are not guided by a common *modus operandi,* however. There is a set of "silent rules" by which the typical asshole operates. Some of these silent rules are:

- All problems are caused by other people.
- It is never necessary to solve problems; just find someone to blame for them.
- All faults and shortcomings can be hidden behind the mask of rudeness. The more at fault you are, the more rude you should be.
- All rules are made to be broken, but only by you. If someone else breaks a rule, blow the whistle on him immediately.
- If you ever run out of rules to use, invent one to suit your needs—and then break it as soon as it no longer serves your purpose.
- Never doubt your ability to attain whatever you want through bullshit.

My own definition of asshole and assholism builds on these many observations. Assholes are people who think they are a law unto themselves—a new species that has the right to do anything they want. Assholism is the disease that infects the value system of these people and enables them to act in the world without a properly functioning conscience or ability to feel guilt, shame, or contrition.

Is assholism truly a disease? At this point, I think we can definitely state, "Yes!" It is an addiction to rudeness and the exploitation of others. Once it takes hold, the average asshole is at its mercy. An asshole simply can't let other people alone. He feels impelled to nag and bitch and ridicule others.

Another indication that assholism is a disease and must be treated as such is its progressive nature. If left untreated, the problem of assholism deepens. In business, for instance, middle management assholes try to become vice-presidential assholes. This is an immense social problem. Suddenly, someone who has the power only to make one hundred people miserable every day of the week may be promoted and given the opportunity to make one thousand people miserable on the same schedule.

The difficulty of treating assholism, of course, is that the typical asshole denies that he is one. Even if he eventually begins to realize that he has been an asshole, he's apt to blame someone else for his behavior. It is not enough just to treat the outer symptoms of rudeness and intimidation, therefore. Such efforts will simply produce a more refined and skillful generation of assholes—assholes who are immune to all criticism and restraints.

No, we must learn to treat the underlying value system; we must reconnect the asshole with his long-abandoned conscience. We must jump start his human decency. This can be a long, hard struggle.

The downside of treating assholes is that the disease is highly contagious. Even a therapist with a strong focus in values and ego strength can easily be infected by the defensiveness and rationalizations of the asshole—to a point where he or she begins to act like an asshole, too!

It is for this reason that we must bring assholism out of the dark shadows of taboo and expose it to the light of day. We must not shrink from calling an asshole an asshole, because it is exactly this kind of professional timidity that allows assholes to fester.

For far too long, assholism has been the disease that dare not speak its name! The time has come, at last, to have the courage to accept assholism for what it is, and begin treating it.

If we will not do it for ourselves, then we must do it for all future generations. Asshole No More!

ACTIVITY

1. Have you ever behaved like an asshole?

2. Is there someone you despise and would like to humiliate or destroy? Write a page or two in your notebook about this person. Then, review what you have written. How do you feel about being an asshole?

4

The Essence of Assholism

I'm OK, but you're an asshole.
—Cardinal Pushing

Although two recovering assholes may disagree on the definition of assholism—in fact, it's almost guaranteed that they will—they can nevertheless agree that they are both assholes. And so they can discuss ideas, feelings, and issues that they have in common. These are the various factors which go together to comprise the essence of assholism.

It is useful to list these factors, so that we can more readily see what an asshole is. Nonetheless, before I actually present these checklists to you, I want to emphasize a very important point. In reading through these lists, you may discover you are an asshole and didn't know it. This is good. It doesn't mean you are a rotten, worthless person, or that you are defective in some way. It just means you are an asshole. Recognizing this gives you the chance to recover.

Assholes should not be blamed for being assholes, any more than a child with the mumps should be blamed for infecting the whole school. Assholes

48

have contracted a disease from which society recoils, but they can be healed. The sooner the problem is detected, the easier recovery will be.

Some assholes contract the disease from their parents, who were assholes themselves. Others are infected later in life, by asshole bosses and asshole wives or husbands. Some are the victims of bad religion. Others took classes in assertiveness training. Other cases are harder to trace, but often have their origins in listening to punk rock, watching TV soap operas, or tuning into C-span.

People become assholes because asshole behavior seems to work. Most young journalists start out as decent human beings, for instance. But after they have seen a nationally-famous TV journalist shove aside thirty people in order to get to a story first, they, too, become infected. Another asshole is born.

Because society rewards people who get there first, assholes seem to prosper. In business, it is often the person who is best at stealing ideas who gets the promotion. In government, it is usually the person who ignores the needs of the public with the most finesse who rises to the top. New generations see assholes succeeding, and stupidly expose themselves to infection.

The problem is that once you become an asshole, you never know where to draw the line. Shoving people aside becomes an addiction, not just an occasional necessity. Sooner or later, the asshole is going to shove the wrong person aside—like a more experienced asshole—and his carefully constructed empire of matchsticks will come tumbling down.

The sordid truth is that most assholes are barely

surviving in their careers and their marriages. It often takes 20 to 30 years for the seeds of destruction to flourish, but they are sown the very first day you cave into pressure and become an asshole. As therapist Ivan Horney puts it, "The asshole takes care of his needs by finding someone else to take care of them for him. But when that person finally wises up and stops propping up the asshole, the entire world caves in on him."

The asshole tries to control his life by controlling the lives of everyone around him. He never solves a problem on his own—he just hides it by raising a big stink about someone else's problems. Eventually, all of these efforts to hide behind a smokescreen fail, and the accumulated problems of two or three decades of being an asshole become apparent.

The asshole, in short, is someone who does the wrong thing in the wrong way for the wrong reason. Let's examine some of these traits and hallmarks more closely.

Caretaking

Assholes are excellent caretakers—they make sure there is always some poor sucker around to take care of them. In business, this is the kind of boss who believes that your sole purpose in life is to support him, make him look good, and take the blame for all of his mistakes. In government, it is the kind of supervisor who will hire two people to do the work he's paid for, so he doesn't have to do anything at all.

Assholes:

• believe that everyone else is put on this world to tend to their needs and make them happy.

- meddle in everyone else's affairs.
- get annoyed when others think for themselves.
- get even more annoyed when anyone expects them to think for themselves.
- view duty as a personal insult. Children, for instance, are inconveniences that get in the way.
- are delighted when other people have problems; it gives them an excuse for their own failures.
- expect everyone else to anticipate their needs, even if it requires mind reading.
- express care by reminding others of their immense debt to them.
- take care of others in such a way that they will never ask for help again.

High Self-Esteem

Since assholes are experts at shirking responsibility and ignoring reality, they have a high self-esteem. Charles Cumberbund, a psychologist at San Quentin, says, "You can't imagine how arrogant assholes can be. If the Queen of England were to inspect the prison, and walk by the cell of an asshole, he would believe she was lucky to have met him." Assholes:
- say "thank you" when you call them an asshole.
- believe they are God's gift to the world.
- believe everyone wants to hear their opinion about everything.
- feel it is their God-given right to condemn any one who has a different opinion than they do.
- are experts at spending other people's money.
- are experts on any subject you can name.
- love to make other people squirm.
- tell themselves they never make mistakes.

- are always able to find someone else to blame for their mistakes.
- expect to be adored if not worshipped.
- inflate their own self-esteem by ridiculing others.
- name their children after themselves.

Repression
Assholes never suffer from repression, except when they are repressed by an even bigger asshole.

Aggression
Assholes are aggressive in all they do. They are aggressive in war, aggressive in peace, aggressive in prayer, and aggressive in saying, "I love you." Of course, in the latter instance, they are usually talking to themselves in the mirror.

Assholes become aggressive when:
- they get out of bed in the morning.
- they feel their control of others slipping away.
- they are criticized.
- they get behind the wheel of their car.
- they get caught with their hand in the till.
- their authority is challenged.
- their BMW is repossessed.

Obsession
All assholes are obsessed with remaining an asshole—with justifying their rudeness and refining their deviousness. They dare not let their guard down for even a minute, lest old traces of innate decency or a smoldering spark of conscience should resurface and force them to confront themselves.

Assholes therefore are obsessed about:

- their ability to appear tough and in control.
- their image. After all, once you get beyond the image, there is nothing there at all.
- being sure there is always someone else to blame. This is one of the primary reasons why many assholes marry and have children.
- their enemies and what they are doing.
- their friends and what they are doing.
- maintaining a strict accounting of all the favors everyone owes them.
- making sure they are never mistaken for an ordinary person.
- making sure everyone knows that their BMW is better than the next door neighbor's.

Rudeness

When assholes talk about the range of their self-expression, they are merely describing the many different ways they have found to be rude. To the asshole, to live is to be rude. Assholes:

- never wait in lines for anything. They always find a way to sneak in.
- never ask. They always demand.
- never praise anyone, unless they want to humiliate their children by praising a friend in their presence, and then add: "Why can't you do as well as this?"
- speak only in one tone of voice: sarcastic.
- will shout only if they don't think it is necessary to scream.
- delight in making your business their business.
- will never pick a fight with you unless you fight back first.

- will stop at the scene of an accident only if they are pinned in their car.
- believe that etiquette is a set of rules designed to give them an advantage over other people.
- believe that if they can't say anything good about someone else, it's been a good day.

Being in Control

Most assholes live to control others. They are therefore terrified by the thought of losing control, either of their own lives or of the lives of people they have got under their thumb. To perpetuate this sense of being in control, assholes:

- make up rules about what others can and cannot do.
- expect everyone to obey these rules—except themselves.
- constantly change the rules, so that only they know for sure what is current policy. This makes it easy to blame others whenever necessary.
- seek to be appointed to positions of power, usually by sucking up.
- surround themselves with sycophantic assistants who enjoy kissing ass.
- love to remind you that they are in charge.
- teach their children that their only reason for being is to enhance the image of their parents.

Humor

The most painful moment an asshole can endure is when social moments require them to be of good humor and cheer. I once invited an asshole aunt of mine over for Christmas dinner. Upon being greeted with "Merry Christmas," she proceeded to give me ten reasons why she wasn't the least bit merry.

Assholes can:

- sneer
- jeer
- laugh at the misfortune of others
- laugh when they get away with something
- tear each other up sarcastically—

but they have no genuine sense of humor, and no capacity to laugh at themselves or a cause they happen to embrace.

Denial

Assholes raise the practice of denial to an art form—in some cases, perhaps even a pagan religion. Whatever you claim, they will deny it. This is therefore one of the few known ways to reliably trap assholes. Tell them the opposite of what you want them to admit, and they will deny it, thereby trapping themselves in reality. Assholes:

- believe that they have no problems or faults.
- believe that they never make mistakes.
- pretend that they never cause problems.
- will deny having said anything that can now be used against them.
- complain about the rudeness of anyone who criticizes them.
- see no need to be consistent. Assholes do not have double standards—they have as many standards as a situation requires.
- will never give you a straight answer.
- believe that truth is just a matter of personal convenience.
- think that "ethics" is a word describing people from foreign countries.

Intimidation

Assholes love to enslave other people. The day the South lost the Civil War, and slavery became illegal, is a day of mourning for all assholes. But the picture has brightened somewhat since then for assholes. They have discovered that it is still possible to enslave and intimidate other people emotionally and mentally, without physically restraining them or breaking the law. In fact, one measure of assholism is the number of people an asshole can successfully intimidate at any given point in time.

Assholes:
* expect other people to make them happy.
* enslave anyone stupid enough to try it.
* are threatened by any asshole who tries to steal someone they have already enslaved.
* dress for intimidation.
* always strive to be an equal opportunity offender.
* cried when Idi Amin was deposed.
* think Captain Queeg was a role model for the ideal boss.
* believe *Mommie Dearest* is a guide to good parenting.

Love

For assholes, life is just one long, uninterrupted love affair with themselves. As one of my patients put it, "The one and only commandment of the asshole is to love himself. And when you get done doing it, you want to do it all over again." There is only one problem. Since assholes by nature cannot love anyone else, except as an aspect of their self-love, their understanding of love is very limited and one dimensional. They know how to forgive, for example—but only themselves. The thought of forgiving someone else, when you could carry a grudge instead, would be utterly alien to the asshole. The love of an asshole creates a very tiny universe, populated by one person and excluding everyone and everything else.

Assholes love:
- themselves.
- their possessions.
- wealth.
- their status.
- their car.
- their knowledge (if intellectual).
- their opinions.
- their prejudices.
- to hate. This is especially true of self-righteous assholes—assholes with a cause.

Assholes covet:
- everything which is not theirs.
- power.
- fame.

Sacrifice

This is a word that is not in the working vocabulary of most assholes, except in the sense of other people capitulating to their demands. Never ask an asshole to give up anything he or she has, even if it is in the asshole's best interest. Assholes are constitutionally incapable of giving up anything. For instance, if you ask an asshole, "Could you help me out by taking these two tickets to the ball game off my hands?" he will have to refuse you, because you are asking him to do you a favor. The proper way to phrase the request is: "Listen, I was thinking about asking you to go to the ball game with me tonight, but I promised my kid I would take him. You don't mind, do you?" Within two minutes, he will have wheedled both tickets from you—even if it means he has to change his plans in order to use them.

Communication

Assholes love to talk, especially about themselves. They are also masters at the art of saying what they have to say in the most confusing, vague manner possible. In this way, it is easy to deny any responsibility for misunderstandings or misstatements. An asshole politician, for instance, will have no compunction about changing the meaning of something he or she said half a dozen times, to fit the current opinions of the public.

The finest hour for any asshole is to be asked to explain the rules or give instructions for some project or program. He knows how to say as little as possible and yet appear to be covering all likely options. This gives him the opportunity to add clarifications after everyone has screwed up, thereby making them look like idiots for not understanding him in the first place. In this way, the asshole cleverly retains complete control over a situation he's not even involved in, and keeps everyone else in a constant state of frustration and irritation.

When assholes communicate, they:
• blame.
• bully.
• don't say what they mean.
• don't mean what they say.

- don't know what they mean.
- don't care if anyone else knows, either, so long as everyone else believes that they do.
- lie to protect themselves.
- lie to ruin someone else.
- lie for the fun of it.
- lie out of habit.
- twist the facts.
- make up facts and statistics that are not true.
- are always true to their feelings, so long as their feelings are primarily anger, irritation, and indignation.
- never ask anyone for his opinion, unless they want to steal an idea.
- protest loudly whenever they feel they have been abused or victimized.
- change the subject quickly whenever anyone else feels they have been abused or victimized—especially by the asshole.

Listening

Assholes are good listeners. They are experts at discovering the weaknesses and vulnerabilities in their friends, colleagues, and enemies, so that they can take advantage of this information at the proper time. They also delight in hearing other people praise them. Beyond this, however, they tend not to hear a thing.

Tolerance

Assholes like to know exactly where they stand—and where they want to stand is on top of the mountain, with everyone else down in the valley. As long as you stay in the place they have assigned you, they will be perfectly tolerant of you. But if you try to climb the mountain, or even think of displacing them, you will inexorably upset the delicate balance the asshole has created. This, of course, is your fault—not theirs.

Assholes love boundaries. They also love walls. They use boundaries at work, to warn colleagues and competitors not to infringe on their territory. They use walls in their personal life, to insure that spouses and children can't get too close to them, and notice how rotten they actually are.

Assholes will tolerate just about anything, so long as it fits naturally into either their boundaries or their walls, or both. It's a small world, isn't it?

To an asshole, tolerance means:

• you should be ready to put up with anything they might do.

• you must be ready to make allowances for their rigid ideas and expectations.

• whatever went wrong, it's your fault.

• anyone who gets in the way must be removed.

Trust

The only thing you can trust assholes to do is to lie, cheat, and scheme whenever they think it is in their best interest—and even if it isn't. As for the ability of assholes to trust others, they don't. It's a lonely life, but they always have their superior wit and charm to comfort themselves.

Anger

The one thing assholes are exceptionally good at is being angry. They are not just in touch with their anger—they are regularly massaged by it. An asshole believes that anger is the only proper way to cope with this hostile and dangerous world in which we live. His motto is: "Never give a sucker an even break—always make sure it is a compound fracture."

Assholes become angry when:

- they wake up in the morning.
- the morning paper arrives late, even though they are not subscribers.
- their coffee is cold.
- others fail to do exactly as they are told to do.
- others do exactly what they are told to do, but it backfires on the asshole.
- they don't know what they want.
- others fail to anticipate what the asshole wants even though he doesn't know it himself.
- it is raining outside.
- it is sunny outside.
- someone takes exception to something they have said.
- someone catches them in an inconsistency.
- there is no one to blame for the mess they have made.
- someone tries to blame the asshole for something he did.
- a friend asks them for a loan.
- a friend tries to collect on a loan.
- others expect them to behave responsibly.
- their children act like children.
- their children try to act like adults.
- others expect them to try to act like adults.
- their spouses get tired of faking affection.
- the person they are having an affair with gets tired of faking affection.

Sex

Most assholes, of both sexes, find it is easier to masturbate than accommodate the needs and desires of a partner. Nonetheless, even an asshole can tell the difference between a fantasy and the real thing. So they try to have a normal sex life.

To an asshole, this means:

• they will have sex, but refuse to enjoy it. This applies primarily to women.

• they will have sex, but refuse to let their partner enjoy it. This applies primarily to men.

• they will use sex as a way of controlling their partner, generally by faking a headache.

• they will use sex as a way of punishing their partner, generally by faking an orgasm.

• the sex is unimportant, just so long as they get to play with whips and chains.

• they will have sex, but never talk about it.

• they will talk about sex, but never have it.

• they will mutually decide to be celibate, as their way of getting even with life.

• they will mistake the word "promise" for the word "promiscuity."

Bitching

Assholes make the world's greatest nags. In her book, *The Art of Bitching*, Naomi Gadfly writes that anyone can complain about the imperfection and chaos of life, but it takes a true asshole to bitch about things that ordinary people find okay, even desirable. "On a spring day the rest of us might rate a perfect ten, the asshole will still be able to find fault. He will bitch that he has to be inside working on such a lovely day, that it is impossible

62

to enjoy days like this when you are married to a bitch like his spouse, or that the birds chirping outside his window are giving him a headache."

Assholes bitch about:
- the amount of money other people make.
- the amount of money they make.
- the fact that they have to work in order to get paid.
- how long it's been since they got laid.
- the weather.
- the economy.
- how little time their adult children spend with them.
- how demanding their parents are. "Didn't we put them in the nursing home so we wouldn't have to visit them?"
- how they were cheated in Granddad's will.
- world politics, even though they don't care about them.
- how no one seems to really like them.
- people who are always bitching.

Sharing

Assholes love to share. They take pride in their generosity, and in the way they share so freely with associates and family members. For example, they are always ready to share:
- their misery.
- the blame.
- responsibility.
- their gloomy outlook on life.
- stress.
- gossip.
- their opinions.

63

- a case of herpes.

There are only a few things assholes do not like to share. These include:
- praise.
- authority.
- money.
- their time.
- moments of triumph or success.
- opportunities.
- good ideas.
- friendship.
- the limelight.
- a kind word.

Paradoxes and Puzzles

Assholes are often a puzzle to others as well as themselves. They are as full of contradictions as a porcupine selling balloons. This is due primarily to the tendency of the asshole to hide behind self-deceptions and inconsistencies. The cumulative effect of this behavior leads to a condition in which they do not know who they are or what they believe in. Assholes:

- claim to be highly responsible and honest, usually when breaking a promise or lying.
- claim to be able to stand on their own, as long as you pay their bills for them.
- want everyone to adore them, so long as they don't get too close.
- claim it's "for your convenience" when they suddenly change plans you've already agreed on.
- will never be more strongly opinionated than when they are talking about topics they know absolutely nothing about.

• claim to love God and hate the devil, whereas it is clear from their behavior that they ignore the former while courting the latter.

The Pooped Out Asshole

Like any addiction, assholism takes its toll on our vitality over the years. It is easy for a twenty-five-year-old to be an asshole; it is a lot harder for the same person to continue all the pretenses, shams, and schemes of assholism twenty years later. It is in this way that Life wears them down, and gradually convinces them that there must be a better way than continuing life as an asshole. Hallmarks of the waning stages of assholism include:

• they become too tired to bitch all the time.
• they don't believe their own bullshit anymore.
• they start writing letters to "Dear Abby."
• they become obsessed with the final years of Howard Hughes.
• they have more frequent fantasies of the complete destruction of their enemies.
• they have a growing realization that many people don't like them.
• they have a growing realization that even those people who say they like them, don't.
• they have the growing suspicion, "Gee, I may be an asshole."

It is impossible to draw up a complete list of all of the hallmarks of assholism. Like any sick person, the asshole behaves in a variety of ways. Not every asshole you know will exhibit all of these characteristics. But these are the most common signs of assholism in human life today.

The important thing is for assholes to be able to see for themselves that they are, indeed, assholes. In order to be ready for recovery, the asshole must see that his problems are not due to other people and circumstances beyond his control. They are due to his own diseased perspective on life.

As Alice Goober puts it in her wonderful book, *Assholes Are Contagious,* one good asshole can easily keep ten to twenty other people in a frenzy of hostility, guilt, or confusion. Many neurotics and depressed people are nothing more than the victims of assholes. The asshole may in fact complain that he is surrounded by nothing but neurotics and angry people, but he is overlooking the fact that it is his own acts that drove them to this behavior!

It is therefore not advisable for the asshole to divorce his wife or disown his kids—or chuck one job for another. Once established in a new situation, the asshole will quickly make the new crew of people as crazy as the last set. No, assholism can only be treated in one way. The asshole must recognize that he or she is sick and infecting everyone else. The spiral will simply continue and renew itself, until the asshole accepts responsibility for the cure. He must stop being an asshole and learn to be a decent human being—a DHB.

Recovery can be fun. It may sound strange to the average asshole, but life is much more enjoyable without the anger, cheating, lying, and scheming all assholes engage in. At first, the asshole is confused, lost. All he is aware of is how empty his life has been. But then, this sense of emptiness recedes and is replaced by a new sense of purpose—a sense of humanity.

Eventually there comes a day when the asshole looks himself in the mirror and actually sees something other than emptiness. He sees humanity, talent, and skill—and he knows he has rediscovered something important. It may not actually be himself, of course—it is probably the reflection of his wife or kids looking over his shoulder. But just being able to see them in the same mirror as himself is a gigantic step in the right direction. It is a message of hope and promise.

ACTIVITY

1. Review the lists contained in this chapter. Mark each trait with a 2 if it is a common trait for you, a 1 if it is intermittent, and a zero if it never occurs. Add your score. If it is over 100, then you ought to consider taking up deep sea diving or moving to Antarctica.

2. Make the same review for each of your best friends. If they all score over 100 as well, you may want to ponder the old adage, "Like attracts like."

3. If someone were to write your biography, how many people would accept it as a plausible story, and how many would think it was a cheap rip-off of a soap opera?

5
Intensities of Assholism

He was an asshole for all seasons—
between the sheets or on the streets,
holding the fort or winning in court.
—from *Life Among the Assholes*

Of course, if you want to put your finger on what
an asshole is, it's not enough just to list its many
and varied symptoms. Being a disease, assholism
is a force that sweeps through human life, infecting
those who are vulnerable. Until we understand
this basic facet of assholism, we will not be able to
approach its treatment wisely.

In many ways, in fact, assholism is like the wind.
The wind can blow forcefully or calmly, continuously or intermittently. It may only ruffle our hair,
or strike savagely in a storm. Occasionally, it un-
leashes a hurricane or tornado and wreaks havoc.

Like the wind, assholes often behave themselves and do not bother anyone else. But when the
right occasion arises, they can quickly lash out with
frightful ferocity. To understand assholism, therefore, it is important to be able to recognize the various intensities of assholism, and how assholes

learn to modulate their self-expression—and even hide behind an outer expression of decency.

It is sometimes difficult for non-assholes to conceive of assholism as a force. Human beings are so oriented to tangible reality! But as a person develops vulnerability to assholism, by surrendering to the inner impulse to be petty, it is almost as though an overpowering force moves in and takes up residence in the household of his character. It begins to tell him what to do, and how to do it. At first, the average person resents this intrusion. But after twenty minutes or so, he gives up and doesn't pay any more attention to it. He just accepts the force of assholism as part of himself. In time, he even learns to trust it.

Among assholes, the equivalent of hurricane or tornado force would be *the flaming asshole*. This is the most flamboyant, obnoxious kind—the type of asshole regularly portrayed in movies and on TV as mean, vicious, and hard-nosed. The flaming asshole is a seemingly inexhaustible source of irritation, aggravation, and destruction. In fact, when portrayed on TV, he is usually so militant that he ends up bringing about his own destruction by the end of the show. He dies the kind of death that only an asshole would ever deserve.

In real life, flaming assholes seldom go around assassinating their enemies, at least with machine guns or bombs. They tend to specialize more in character assassination. But they still have an enormous capacity to be obnoxious, mean, rude, and exploitative day in, day out.

John was a person who worked for a flaming asshole. He was told one week that he had to prepare a special report and have it ready the following Monday. He worked all weekend to make sure the report was done, and had it on his boss's desk at 8 a.m. Monday morning. Five minutes later his boss buzzed him on the intercom.

"This report was due on Friday," his boss barked. "It's worthless to me now."

"But you told me it was due this morning," John replied.

"Are you suggesting it's all my fault?" his boss asked.

"Not at all, sir," John replied. "I guess I misunderstood what you said."

"Make sure it never happens again," his boss barked, then hung up.

John always tried to do exactly what his boss told him to do, but it was never good enough. He was kept in a constant state of terror, fearing the wrath of his boss, even though his work was impeccable and his boss depended on him to do two jobs— his and John's both.

The best way to deal with flaming assholes is to stay as far away as possible. If this is not possible, then do as John has learned to do—to treat them with the utmost care.

Do not count on them to self-destruct. These people have tremendous stamina and staying power. They don't *get* headaches or ulcers—they *give* them! They seem to survive forever. These are the people about whom it is said, "God doesn't want them, and the devil is afraid to take them." So, we're stuck with them.

A step down in intensity from the flaming asshole is *the situational asshole.* These people are like

70

the breeze on a hot, humid day—it is pleasant for the most part, but a sudden gust can blow your hat right off your head. They can be good neighbors and co-workers when they put their mind to it— they know how to be generous, kind, cooperative, and decent—if it is in their best interest. Their assholism only flashes at intervals—when they are provoked or acting under a great deal of stress. Otherwise, they seem to be ordinary people.

Edith was a classic case of the situational asshole. A young mother, she handled the stresses and challenges of motherhood admirably in almost all circumstances. She would support her young off-spring with kind and nurturing words, and was always there to help them deal with the usual child-hood traumas and pains. But one day she was un-usually testy. She had just told her kids for the third time that day to clean up their toys. When she came back into the playroom fifteen minutes later, the toys were still strewn across the floor. So she gathered them all up, stuffed them in a couple of boxes, and hauled the toys—and the kids—down to the Salvation Army, where she made a big spectacle of donating each and every last toy of theirs to charity, forcing her kids to watch. The kids cried for four days after that, but she showed no pity. She told them that if they wanted new toys, they would have to earn the money for them on their own. So far, though, the three-year-old has not been able to find a steady source of income.

The most subdued level of assholism is *the sissy asshole.* This is not to suggest that they are any less dangerous than the flaming asshole—they just aren't visible in the dark. Having seen the way society responds to flaming assholes, sissy assholes choose to hide behind a façade of apparent meekness and politeness. But they still know how to stick in the knife and turn it, and often without anyone realizing it was they who did it.

The sissy asshole is like the wind on a spring evening. It feels lovely, but what you don't realize is that you are in the process of catching a cold that will last half way through the summer.

It is possible to be around sissy assholes for years and not even realize that they are assholes. Outwardly, they may be gracious, friendly, flattering, generous, perhaps even pious. They say all the right words and do all the right things. But this is actually just a well-rehearsed act to beguile you into trusting them. Behind your back, they are conjuring up all the usual asshole tricks.

Sissy assholes are often passive-aggressive. They do much of their harm by errors of omission—that is, they fail to do things they would ordinarily be expected to do, to your detriment. Their profession of concern for your well-being often sounds as though they were Mother Theresa in the flesh, except that they never follow through with any tangible assistance.

Dr. Rhoid, in *Assholes Among Us*, writes: "Some assholes do all their damage by default. They don't need to lie, cheat, rage, or bully. They achieve their ends just by letting you down at critical moments, or distracting your attention from duties you need to be performing, and will be blamed for if you do not."

There are two basic kinds of sissy assholes—the sweet and the sour. The sweet type is an art form unto itself. To your face, these assholes are all sweetness and flattery. They are sometimes so sweet it seems almost too good to be true—and it is! These people are concerned about everything that happens to you and will grieve with you over all your losses. In fact, they will gladly exaggerate those losses for you. They will gradually turn you into the most depressed person in your neighborhood, crying about everything from sad-sounding song birds to limping cockroaches, until you are totally disabled and completely dependent upon them for guidance and direction.

The sweet sissy asshole is often found in churches. Bob is a minister who told this story at a recent meeting of Assholes Non-Anonymous.

One evening, Bob was scheduled to conduct a staff meeting at his church, but at the last minute was called downtown to attend a special meeting the bishop had arranged to discuss aid for the homeless. He dispatched his assistant, the Rev. Caroline Tittsworthy, to handle the staff meeting in his stead. One of the members attending the meeting commented on Bob's absence *once again*. The Rev. Tittsworthy's reply was a classic comment by a sweet sissy asshole: "We must pray for Bob's shortcomings."

Bob heard of this slam the next day via the grapevine. When he confronted Caroline afterwards, she was all smiles and apologies, claiming that she had been misunderstood and misquoted. "What I said," she replied sweetly, "is that you were away, but would be coming back shortly."

The coating of honey that drips from their deceit makes it very hard to catch a sweet sissy asshole.

And even if you do, they make sure you get covered with as much of their slime as possible.

The sour sissy asshole is more like a lap cat who is friendly and purring while in your lap, but a trained killer in your back yard. You look at him and wonder how an adorable creature like that could possibly be so bloodthirsty.

Sour sissy assholes are jealous of anyone who is happier, more successful, or more talented than they are. As a result, they will very quietly brew up a nice pot of dissension. They frequently appoint themselves as guardians of family unity, so that they can methodically poison the family atmosphere and turn brother against sister, parent against child, and uncle against cousin.

They also often emerge as guardians of morality and purity, almost always on utterly petty points. They are therefore a fountain of gossip, and while they would never call it gossip, because gossip is a sin, they nonetheless deal openly in the bartering of the reputations of others.

Like other modern-day puritans, sour sissy assholes often pose as models of virtue. But this is mainly an illusion created with smoke and mirrors. Their intense interest in the failings of others is meant to misdirect attention away from their own failings and imperfections.

Should you actually get the goods on a sour sissy asshole, you are apt to become the target of a lecture on humility and forgiveness. But God help you if you ever need to ask forgiveness from this same type of person. You will receive a quick course on what it means to be damned with faint forgiveness!

The effort to describe these differing intensities

of assholism is not meant to confuse anyone, or to suggest that assholes are always of one intensity or another. Even the flaming asshole will have days when he or she seems to behave like a decent person; given a good job or a supportive family, he might calm down and become a situational asshole. A sweet sissy asshole may turn into a sour one if tired or cornered.

Instead, these differing levels of intensity have been discussed for a very important reason. Studies have shown that when the average person hears the word, "asshole," he or she thinks only of the flaming variety. This cripples them in learning to deal with situational or sissy assholes. It may also delay many people from realizing that they are themselves assholes, even though they do not particularly flame.

Whether your own interest in assholes is private or as part of a recovery workshop, it is important to realize that not all assholes use the same strategies and schemes. Their goals are the same, and the nature of their character will be similar. But the actual means for getting what they want out of life may differ greatly.

You may not think these distinctions matter. But if we cannot split assholes into these categories, we will never be sure how to proceed in treating them. As some asshole once said, "If you aren't part of the solution, you are part of the problem."

Only the recovering asshole knows how true that statement is.

ACTIVITY

1. What kind of asshole are you?
2. Have you ever personally been blown away by the full force of an asshole?
3. If a flaming asshole married a sour sissy asshole, what kind of children would they produce?

Part Two:
Varieties of Assholes

6
The Run-of-the-Mill Asshole

Sometimes, I just stay up late at night and wonder—were assholes developing on this planet while the rest of us were evolving? Or did they come from some other planet—like Uranus?
—Erica, victim of family assholes

The disease of assholism embraces a vast range of cultural types—or at least half-vast. Unfortunately, all too many authorities limit their discussion of assholism to the flaming asshole. They describe the asshole in its most conspicuous forms—at work, as a social protestor, in government, and in religion. There is, of course, a lot to be said about each of these varieties of asshole, as we will see in later chapters. But many of these authorities overlook the most common asshole of all—the run-of-the-mill asshole that is to be found at the mall, on the freeway, in movie theaters, next to you in bed, or at family reunions.

It is sometimes hard to distinguish run-of-the-mill assholes from the average person, even though they do exhibit all the usual asshole characteristics. This is primarily because they are cleverly disguised as ordinary people, and we accept them as such. They deftly hide behind social conventions and work hard to convince us that if they push and shove a bit, or scheme and connive, it is no worse than what everyone else is doing.

They are also highly skilled in taking advantage of our own inhibitions. These include:

1. We may be related to them, and therefore less inclined to view them as assholes. You may be reluctant, after all, to think that your own mother might have given birth to an asshole.

2. We may have selected them as friends all on our own, and are therefore less than eager to admit that we made a mistake. No one enjoys confessing: "I married an asshole." It tends to cast a shadow of doubt on the quality of our judgment.

3. We may have only infrequent contact with some of these people. Unless we are an asshole ourself, we are probably reluctant to conclude that a waiter at a local restaurant is an asshole just on the basis of one or two instances. We are willing to give people the benefit of the doubt.

4. We want to think that most people are normal, decent human beings. Actual experience tells us otherwise: the majority of people are assholes. But the idea that we are evolving *beyond* the monkeys and apes, and not back *toward* them, is a strong precept in the human imagination.

Still, in spite of all these natural inhibitions, there are times when we must come to the inescapable conclusion: so-and-so is an asshole.

Aunt Mary is a flaming asshole.

Cousin Jack is a dickhead.

The manager of the movie theater is a situational asshole: he threw you out last year when he heard someone talking during the film and thought it was you, but he gave you a free pass when he later discovered he was wrong.

The clerk at the post office is a sour sissy asshole.

Your son's teacher is a sweet sissy asshole.

My own research has indicated that family situations provide the ripest opportunities for assholism. This is especially true at family reunions—large gatherings of aunts, uncles, grandparents, and cousins who haven't seen one another for twenty-five years and don't care to see each other now, except that one or two scheming assholes have decided that the family has been apart for far too long and ought to get back together again. Everybody knows perfectly well why the family hasn't gotten together for twenty-five years, but no one has the courage to bring the subject up. So, seventy-five to one hundred people who have nothing in common except their dislike for one another all congregate in the same spot for one disastrous weekend, just to make two flaming assholes happy and increase their manipulative powers.

A smaller version of this scenario plays itself out on a more regular basis, usually at birthdays and Christmas. One devoted offspring will hold a birthday party for his or her parents, and everyone else in the family is expected to attend, even if it means flying in from out of state. Having another obligation is never accepted as a valid excuse, and if you have the chutzpah to dare miss the occasion, the birthday parent is bound to contribute to the mischief by remarking out loud, "Oh, I only wish that so-and-so (that's you!) could have been here!"

These miniature dramas of ordinary family life are classic examples of assholism at work. The person who stages the party is seeking to gain control over other family members, by telling them what they are supposed to do—and making them do it. If a simple request does not suffice, they will quickly turn to manipulation and coercion—a phone call from another family member subtly applying pressure. You will, of course, be expected to chip in to help buy the birthday parent a present you would never choose and the parent will never use. If you refuse, then you will be ridiculed and ostracized by everyone else who does contribute—even if you buy a separate gift on your own.

There is only one purpose to these occasions: one person is seeking to enforce conformity on everyone else, all in the name of family unity. The sooner everyone in the family recognizes this is the work of assholes, the better—but few families ever manage to spot these run-of-the-mill assholes. In point of fact, most family assholes thrive with the blessing of the very people they prey upon.

Indeed, this is generally the outstanding feature of all run-of-the-mill assholism—it exists because everyone who is victimized by it nevertheless willingly tolerates it. This may be in part because they do not readily recognize it as assholism, but it is also in part because no one wants to rock the boat. No one wants to make waves. So they just quietly sink instead.

All the while, these assholes adroitly use double

and triple standards to keep everyone else confused, doing to others precisely what they would never tolerate others doing to them. They assume special privileges and rights at the very same time that they deny them to others.

Incidentally, don't fall into the illusion of believing that you can outlast an asshole aunt or uncle. These people never give up—apparently not even after death. Prunella Worthington, the celebrated English medium, writes in *Sixty Years Among the Dead*, that assholes remain as assholes even after they die. In many cases, they refuse to accept the reality of death and remain earthbound, screaming at living relatives who (mercifully) can no longer hear them.

In fact, I had an uncle like that. He would keep returning as a ghost at the most inopportune times. Eventually, the only part of him that returned was his asshole—there wasn't anything else left of the poor fellow.

There never is, once the scourge of assholism has been allowed to do its worst.

ACTIVITY

1. How many assholes can you count among the members of your immediate family? Your extended family? What are their specialties?

2. How regularly do you choose friends who are actually assholes? What does this tell you about the kind of company you seek?

7

The Three-Piece Asshole

"I never saw a dollar I didn't like."
—Bernard Groffstein, a recovering
asshole

Industry, commerce, and business are fields which attract a great many assholes. The reason why is simple: assholes love money, power, and conflict. The profit motive in business appeals to the asshole's love for money. Management gives him a perfect vehicle to abuse power. And competition is the ideal outlet for the asshole's innate destructiveness.

In fact, the history of business is filled with assholes. The tombs of the ancient pharaohs contained papyrus scrolls with titles such as *Winning through Genocide* and *The One-Minute Asshole.* Another ancient text, *Management Hints of Genghis Khan,* lists four steps to becoming what it called "the top brasshole"—1) kill all competitors; 2) grab the power for yourself; 3) hide your real intentions behind a screen of lies; and 4) set up your operation so that no one except you knows the full scope of what you are doing. Nor should we ignore the more recent influence into Western business, the "I've Got a Yen" Asshole.

The three-piece asshole can be a master of his craft. After all, the assholes in this league play hard ball. And they play for keeps.

In the ordinary business person, competition is a healthy motive. But in the three-piece asshole, it becomes a bloodthirsty passion. Often referred to by the nickname "Rambo," these assholes are driven by the awareness that "more is never enough." They want every last account in their field and will work relentlessly to get it. But they can never really enjoy their massive triumphs, because they intuitively know that if they rest for even a moment, some other asshole will step in and steal their business from them. They not only want to win and win big, but they can never rest until they see their competition completely squashed.

Just so, sensible people understand the need for power in management and respect it, using it wisely. But in the three-piece asshole, power is only an ego trip. The people who fall into this category believe that the only reason why their company exists is to serve as a personal power base for them. Their lust for power is so great they have earned the sobriquet "Ayatollah." The ego of any asshole is enormous, of course, but the ego of a three-piece Ayatollah is generally the size of the Goodyear blimp, and requires a larger crew to support it. This breed of asshole uses power exclusively to show everyone else who's boss—to fire malcontents, to hire loyal supporters, to challenge the heads of other departments, and to put the screws to everyone working for him. He treats his staff as though they were galley slaves on Africa's Barbary Coast, and has even less respect for his customers, whom he views as potential thorns in his side. His motto is: "The customer is always wrong, unless I happen to be the customer."

The decent business person operates openly, with nothing to hide. But the three-piece asshole would never dream of acting openly. He believes business is one big poker game, and so sets up a smokescreen of lies and deceit behind which he makes all of his moves. The bible of this type of asshole is a book called *The Art of the Steal* by Donald Crump, who writes, "Directness and sincerity are for namby-pambies. The most effective strategy in business has always been management by manipulation. Why take the time to acquire power, talent, and connections through honest hard work, if you can get the same things by stealing them?"

Of course, if you lack talent, power, and ability, you must be able to rely on charm and double-talk to bluff your way through meetings, quarterly evaluations, interviews, and negotiations. This produces the third variety of three-piece asshole, The Blowhard. The Blowhard is at his best when he doesn't have a clue what he's talking about. He knows that style is everything in most business circles, and so if he acts as if he knows everything, everyone else will assume that he does, too. These people see themselves as experts at motivating (bullshitting), resourcefulness (stealing ideas), negotiation (intimidation), and management (covering their ass). Of course, they do not act wholly on their own—the effort to succeed without skill or talent is supported by a four hundred million dollar per year business of books, seminars, and tapes.

The last variety of business asshole is "the MBA," which stands for "Master of Being an Asshole." These are people who are long on theory and short on common sense. They have impressive degrees from the academic world, as well as lots of answers—although no solutions—to every problem that arises. This species of asshole is known for conducting long, boring meetings in which statistics are given more importance than people, products, or the marketplace. They approach all problems as though they are hypothetical situations that can be solved by abstract theories.

Of course, business is a field of high turnover, and every year quite a few three-piece assholes disappear from the scene. It is usually thought that they are fired, but the truth of it is that they simply evaporate into a cloud of their own bullshit.

But even then it may not be the last we hear from them. In many cases, they reappear a year or two later as management consultants.

ACTIVITY

1. Who do you work with who is a three-piece asshole?

2. What tricks has he or she pulled on you in the last six months? Last six days? Last six minutes?

3. Is this person aware of being an asshole? If not, organize a pool in your office to draw lots. The person drawing the shortest stick wins the pleasure of telling this person, on behalf of the entire staff, that he or she is an asshole.

8
The Liberated Asshole

> I never felt fully alive, unless I had
> protested in public at least once a
> week. The cause didn't matter—it
> was the thrill of protest I lived for.
> —Henrietta Brown, recovering ac-
> tivist asshole

The fashion today is to protest social injustice.
First, you discover how society has imprisoned you,
psychologically or socially. Then, you protest, de-
claring that it is your right to be liberated. But most
folks don't wait around for the issue to be decided
rationally. They unilaterally proclaim that they
have been liberated, and begin acting as such. The
odd thing is that they don't seem to believe their
own propaganda, because they continue to protest
as if they had not yet achieved liberation. Of
course, this is not actually a contradiction, for all
they have really accomplished, in most cases, is the
liberation of their previously secret identity as assholes.

In his essay, "The Cry of the Asshole," Peter Lilly
traces the roots of activist assholism from the

drunken brawls of stone age man through the bomb throwing anarchists of the Nineteenth Century and the protest movements of our current times. He warns that the acceptance of protest movements as a legitimate social phenomenon is creating a real threat. Society is well on the way to embracing assholism.

There is much truth to this warning. A large number of the folks who come to me and proclaim, "I am an asshole," received their introduction to assholism as part of the protest marches of the 1960's. In the intervening years, they have learned to protest so well that they have been progressively liberated from marriages, careers, homes, and the respect of their peers. They have also been liberated from peace of mind, money, self-respect, and the vast majority of their friends.

It should be emphasized here that it is not the cause that creates the asshole. It is the thrill of protest for the sake of protest. Few people protesting acid rain, for example, have any idea what acid rain is—or even if it exists. They would protest alkaline rain just as readily, and maybe even both simultaneously. Just the same, there are few people who truly care whether or not whales or seals or owls are preserved for all time. They just want to be identified with the latest, greatest craze. It is the zeal of righteousness that appeals to them—not moral rightness.

The liberated asshole is perhaps the most deadly kind of asshole—not because he is highly vicious, as some of them are, but because he is so highly infectious. Most assholes work alone. The liberated asshole deliberately tries to stage rallies attracting hundreds of thousands of people, all of whom can be relied on to chant some silly slogan in unison in the hopes of changing the world. This is the perfect atmosphere for the spread of assholism.

As Adolf Schneider has put it so eloquently in *Assholes I Have Known,* "Hitler actually won the war. I am not talking about his military campaign, but rather his efforts to make demagoguery popular again. He has spawned a generation of protestors who will stop at nothing to promote their cause, generally at the expense of society. Fascism lives in asshole protests."

This, indeed, is one reason why protest seems to be much more entrenched in the social style of Europe—especially Germany—than in this country, although the U.S. is trying to make up for lost time. Europeans on the whole seem much more blasé about assholism and the need to stop it.

There are five facets to the unique nature of the liberated asshole. They are:

1. Liberated assholes have an amazing ability to see only one side of an issue—their own self-interest. This is why, for example, only whites who discriminate against blacks are racists. Blacks who discriminate against blacks are merely bad neighbors. Blacks who discriminate against whites are "social activists." And blacks who discriminate against Hispanics or Koreans are just taking reasonable steps to preserve the ethnic integrity of the black community. The same kind of one-sided logic has been adopted by feminists, Indians, union sympathizers, and, most recently, the homeless.

2. Liberated assholes love to hate. Their cause becomes a religion—a consecrated activity above

criticism. Opponents therefore instantly become enemies, and anyone who is not with them is against them. They will refuse to listen to any contradictory opinions or facts, lest it might change their minds or challenge their loyalty. But in spite of the ferocity of their hatred, most of these people have spent very little time actually trying to understand their cause.

3. They presume the right to be unfair, obnoxious, and litigious. If you have to kill a few beavers yourself, so you can film it and claim that it was the work of the trapping industry, that's just the price one has to pay for serving the cause. Once you are liberated, you can be as rude and arrogant as you please, because you are, after all, "serving the cause." This presumably gives you the license not only to abuse people verbally in the streets for wearing furs, but also to ruin their private property by spraying paint on expensive fur coats.

4. They lie to themselves as well as everyone else. A typical activist asshole trick is to profess nonviolence and invoke the memory of Gandhi, while massaging class hatreds and unresolved conflicts, so that violence becomes inevitable.

5. Above all, liberated assholes have no sense of humor. If you innocently joke about their sacred cause, you immediately become a demon that must be exorcised. It's as though they have a fear of laughing at themselves, lest the purity of their prejudices be shattered. A Jew can joke about Jewishness, and a black can joke about the ghetto, but a WASP who tries to joke about either will quickly get stung. Instead of Polack jokes, we now make fun of lawyers. But it's highly dubious that

humor that has been racially and sexually sanitized is any funnier—or even more wholesome—than the unliberated variety. Just more censored.

Liberated assholes are afflicted by a terrifying addiction to power. These are people who will not rest until they have achieved full power to tell the rest of us how to live our lives. But the irony is on them: they can only gain their own sense of liberation by enslaving everyone else and forcing them to bow to their whims. Their addiction is, of course, just another form of slavery. They need their victims just as much as their victims do not need them.

As one of my former patients told me, "The only thing I ever loved to do was hate my husband. I'm sorry now that I killed him. My life seems so empty now. It's hard to find anything to do." Fortunately for her—and the rest of us—they keep her busy at the penitentiary now.

ACTIVITY

1. Are you a liberated person? How were you imprisoned? Has your life improved since you were liberated? Or do you just feel conned?

2. Think of as many liberated people as you can. Are any of them happy, contented people? How many need tranquilizers or anti-depressants to get through the day? What lesson can you learn from them?

9
The Holy Asshole

A born-again asshole is still an asshole.
—Rex Havoc,
a recovering fundamentalist asshole

If patriotism is the last refuge of scoundrels, then bad religion may well be the last refuge of assholes. Some even say that the holy asshole *is* the quintessential asshole.

Fortunately, not all religious people are assholes. There is, after all, such a thing as *good* religion, and adherents of these groups do much that is helpful—although probably not enough to neutralize the damage done by the massive hordes of holy assholes. But like anything else, good religion can become bad religion when it falls into the hands of the wrong people:

- Bible-bangers.
- Guilt mongers.
- Bomb throwing Shiite Moslems.
- Almost anyone in Northern Ireland.
- Almost anyone in the Middle East.
- Fundamentalists, be they Christian, Jew, Moslem, or Hindu.

93

The holy asshole towers above all other assholes in two ways. First, they are able to call on *both* God and the devil to terrorize their enemies. They can therefore cloak their malice in divine righteousness and their curses in piety. As one of my recovering patients said, "I used to be really jealous of my pastor. He had God to help him promote guilt and the Devil to help him magnify fear. It was an unfair advantage."

Second, holy assholes believe it is their moral duty to spread their blight to everyone else. Most assholes are private people, who keep their trade secrets to themselves. This is not true of the holy asshole, who actively tries to convert other people into being holy assholes, too. They even do it door to door!

In dealing with holy assholes, of course, we must recognize two classifications:

1. The fanatic holy asshole—the ardent church member who is obviously not getting enough sex and therefore seeks compensation by foisting his or her religious beliefs on everyone else.

2. The professional holy asshole—members of the clergy who happen to be assholes. Although evangelists seem to fit into this group, they actually belong in a separate class—mega-assholes.

It is not necessary to document assholism in evangelists—they expose themselves in the world media frequently enough as it is. But since many good people are probably shocked to learn that their own pastor, and many of the prominent members of their congregation or temple, may well be assholes, it may be helpful to examine the true hallmarks of the holy asshole.

- They are arrogant and righteous. They wouldn't know humility if it bit them in the ass. This, of course, never prevents them from lecturing often on the subject of humility. It is not their own humility they are advocating, after all, but yours—so that you be less tempted to challenge their presumed authority. A little groveling may not be good for the soul, but it sure helps keep the church pews—and the collection plates—full.

- Their way is the one right way, and if you don't acknowledge that, you might as well be dead. In fact, many holy assholes will be willing to help you achieve that goal.

These people will not only use the scripture of their particular faith to beat you over the head, they will also insist that only their narrow, dogmatic interpretation is correct. If you challenge them, then it is obvious that you have been influenced by the Devil.

They will never admit it, of course, but holy assholes are also adept at making up quotes out of thin air and attributing them to scripture. They rely on the fact that believers will never question them, and nonbelievers have too little knowledge of scriptures to know any better. Like all assholes, they assume they can bluff their way through anything.

Professional holy assholes are often hypnotic in their speaking ability. In some cases, their public performances are so powerful they have been known to frighten rabid dogs and wilt geraniums. One of my patients, who used to be a follower of the Rev. Billy Willie, told our group: "He uses words like bullets and bombs. He acts as if God must consult *him* before He takes any major steps."

• They are judgmental and intolerant. Although holy assholes often claim to be guided by the gentleness of Jesus, it is clear from their behavior that tolerance is an endangered species and must be reserved only for unusual circumstances. In point of fact, the holy asshole delights in sniffing at the heels of others, seeking out traces of brimstone. They love to condemn. Even God would have to walk softly and keep His mouth shut to avoid offending a holy asshole. Fortunately, they do not frequent His neighborhood.

In his pamphlet, "The Money in Sanctimony," the Rev. Nasal Robertson claims, "The true Christian must fight the Devil everywhere—in every shadow, under every rock, and in every heart." The wisdom behind this advice is simple: if the true believer is busy fighting the Devil, he won't have the time to notice how much money Nasal is slipping into his own pockets.

• They love sin. They claim to abhor it, of course, but this is just an act. They get their thrills by condemning what they perceive to be the weaknesses of others. They are perverts in convert's robes, yet they are still stained by their fear, malice, self-loathing, and paranoia. This sadism is exemplified by the Rev. Jimmy Braggert, who said, in his commencement address to the graduating class of the Seminary of the All Sinners, Saved or Unsaved, Church of the Holy Brethren:

"I know I haven't done God's work for the day unless I have inspired people to admit their multiple sins and confess their worthlessness. I want to see them cry and beg for forgiveness—to writhe in agony, weep in regret, and experience their total worthlessness. I want them to clean out everything bad, so that they can be born again."

Unfortunately, when holy assholes clean away everything bad, nothing is left. And so all they can do is repeat the cycle over and over again, with an orgy of sin followed by an orgy of repentance. If holy assholes did not invent guilt, hypocrisy, and sin, they certainly perfected them.

ACTIVITY

1. In what ways can atheism be considered a step closer to God than fundamentalism?

2. Has a holy asshole ever come to your door to convert you? Did you let him in? How did you feel after the visit? Reborn? Or full of sinful thoughts?

3. Do you think God believes in you?

10
The New Age Asshole

> Put *this* in your chakras and spin it.
> —Shirley M., flipping the "bird" to a fundamentalist.

Just as the holy asshole can find no good in anyone, there is also a species of person who can find nothing bad in others—or so they claim, until you cross them. These are the children of the New Age. They positively believe that God is bursting out everywhere, making everything and everyone perfect *right now*. It is therefore enough just to be here now.

At first glance, many of these people just seem to be fools—not assholes. They will believe in any freak in a sheet that comes along, with or without Rolls Royces. They are original subscribers to the "Fad of the Month" club, and have probably practiced some form of martial art. They may or may not eat meat, but they most assuredly drink lots of carrot juice and sometimes take their coffee by enema (without sugar, of course). Most of them live in California.

But once you get past the fools, you will find that

many of the people in the New Age are just as big assholes as anyone in the Old Age. For starters, the term "New Age" itself is somewhat arrogant, as applied by its proponents. They reject the Establishment and everything it stands for, preferring to create a whole new utopia where everything is perfect and nothing out of harmony. This, indeed, was a popular idea back in the 1960's. The number of communes still in operation from that time gives a pretty good indication of how well-founded the New Age is.

Actually, nothing in the New Age is new. It is an odd amalgam of ancient ideas and practices, most of which should be left to ancient history.

It may be a good idea to remember that two of the "patrons" of the New Age were Timothy Bleary, a burned-out druggie, and Bagman Rajneesh, a collector of very expensive toys. These are two of the mega-assholes on which many smaller, flaming assholes based their own schemes to milk the New Age.

This is the New Age asshole—the uninspired, unenlightened huckster who can recognize a profitable fad when he sees one, and promote the hell out of it. One year, it may be classes in assertiveness training, the next it may be seminars in past life recall or channeling for fun and mischief. But it preys upon the gullibility of human nature as well as our desire to become better and happier people.

These people hide behind a basic spiel that God is everywhere; all we need to do is to tap into this cosmic connection and we can be in tune with whatever and whomever we desire. If we need money, we just tune in to it and draw it to us. If we need love, the same. We will be able to converge harmonically.

This type of bland belief in the wonderful nature of life is, of course, appealing to many people. But it is very dangerous, because it lets good people be hypnotized by assholes in guru's sheets.

At one point, I thought there was going to be a major breakthrough in the New Age. One popular seminar started out by telling everyone: "You are an asshole." Great! I thought—at last, here is someone who knows how to help people. But it turned out that he was the biggest asshole of all, because the whole class ended up just being a glorification of assholism, not a cure.

One of my favorite books on New Age assholism is *Zen and the Art of Being an Asshole,* by Sidney Koan. This small book really tells it like it has never been. Zen is an ancient Buddhist technique which has gained great popularity in this country. But Zen doesn't teach you anything other than how to be nothing; it is a big putdown. The Zen Master will draw a chalk line on the pavement and then tell his student, "I will give you your next lesson when you have slid under the line."

The intelligent student would pick up the chalk and draw a series of circles on the backside of the Master's robe. When asked the purpose of this, he would reply, "I need a target for sliding under that line."

The typical New Ager is an advocate of niceness and gentleness. If someone is stressed out, the New Ager will gently comfort them and advise them to just let it be. These are the same folks, though, that are building armed camps in Oregon, Montana, and other isolated areas, and are sufficiently armed with modern weapons to be able to put down an uprising in Nicaragua.

Actually, the New Age asshole can be just as smug and righteous as the holy asshole. Not only are many of them heavily into guns and grenades, but many of them openly enlist new recruits. In one notorious instance, the name of the leader is even synonymous with the act of openly displaying one's asshole, but people keep on supporting him and joining his group anyway. In another, the assholes in charge revealed the New Age way to keep the faithful in the flock; anyone who tried to leave would be threatened with dire bodily harm.

Even on an individual basis, New Agers can be as pushy and opinionated as any asshole. Vegetarians are determined to convince the world that it is possible to live on leafy green vegetables and vitamins. Of course, if you look at vegetarians, they almost all look as though they could use a good steak.

Others are certain that creative visualization is the answer to all of life's problems. I have been trying this myself—I have been visualizing that all of the assholes in the world suddenly disappeared. So far, nothing has happened.

One thing New Age assholes have mastered, however, is the art of plagiarism. Probably due to their belief that all things come from God, they will not hesitate to steal ideas—and even whole passages—from others and claim them as their own.

This same level of consciousness—and everything in the New Age is one level of consciousness or another—leads many New Age assholes to view themselves as instant experts on just about any subject. As soon as they see their first aura, you can be sure they will be teaching classes in clairvoyance and related topics.

The ultimate New Age thrill, of course, is subliminal programming. Some asshole who doesn't know what he is doing will prepare a cassette tape of music or just background noise, inserting microsecond messages that cannot be heard by the physical ear but will be detected by the subconscious. By listening to these tapes, you are supposed to be able to overcome doubts and fears, stop smoking, and become a better lover.

I deciphered one of these tapes, but I didn't find the programming that had been advertised. Instead, I found this message: "Hey, asshole—send me an order for at least ten more of these tapes as soon as you can."

ACTIVITY

1. Have you ever been rolfed? Have you ever had your aura balanced? Can you recall your former lives? What were you smoking, and how much?

2. Have you been unsuccessfully trying to win the lottery through visualization? Perhaps you need to call up everyone else doing the same thing and ask them to knock it off for a week.

11
The Bureaucratic Asshole

*Your work is never done until the
clay tablet work is done.*
—head scribe to Persian Emperor
Cyrus V, to his staff

The greatest frustration for any asshole is to feel
that he lacks the power to reach the many people he
longs to control. No asshole ever needs to suffer in
this way, however. The American Way provides the
ideal refuge for every frustrated asshole—working
for a governmental or military bureaucracy. There,
the asshole will find all the clout he or she needs to
control and intimidate unsuspecting, naïve people
who still believe that ours is a "government of the
people, for the people, and by the people." It is actually a government of bureaucratic assholes, dedicated to the proposition of their own comfort.

In her memoirs, *The Joy of Nasty,* Julia Kidds
writes about her career as a petty bureaucrat in the
department of motor vehicles. "Our favorite game
was flunking people who had actually passed.
Sometimes we had them coming back four or five
times to get their license! On the written exam, we

would just mark right answers as being wrong. In the driving test, we would make up laws as we went along. Do you know the law that lets you turn right on red? We made that up just to confuse people. Finally, we had confused so many people, the state had to make it a law. Now, that's real power, I say!"

When interviewed on *3600 Seconds,* Julia was accompanied by her former supervisor, who proudly stated, "Julia was a law unto herself. When she dies, she will probably straighten out God about the disorderly way He makes it rain."

Not all members of all bureaucracies are assholes, of course, although it is a high risk group. There is often long and arduous training—known as military service—required for the choicest spots in government bureaucracies. These, of course, are the positions that deal directly with the general public.

This is most easily seen in the Post Office, Social Security, and the Internal Revenue Service, where it is clear that the number of complaints received about each clerk becomes the basis for future promotions and salary increases—the more complaints received, the better one's chances of advancement.

Capriciousness is likewise obviously rewarded. If the enforcement of rules were consistent, it would make these jobs too boring for the average asshole. It is therefore important to keep the thrill in these desk jobs. "If a fellow is cute, I'll let him off easy," says Ernestine Kabalshinski of the San Diego traffic bureau. "But if he looks like he needs roughing up, I'll throw the book at him. I like to let 'em know they ain't so smart. They have to answer to me."

In his book, *Assholes I Have Known,* Adolph Schneider labels the bureaucratic asshole as a sour-sissy asshole looking for the opportunity to become a situational asshole. These people lack the courage to be a business asshole—or even a politician. But given the protection of the whole government, they are strong enough to take advantage of it. The lowest wimp can become a John Wayne, making the powerless cringe and the innocent appear guilty. Some even become strong enough to qualify as flaming assholes. These are promoted to supervisor or department head.

Time is the most valuable weapon of the bureaucratic asshole. They have plenty of it; you have none. If you are submitting a petition, it was due two weeks ago. If you are applying for a license of any kind, the appropriate office is only open from 6 to 7 a.m. on Thursday mornings. If you need approval before starting some kind of project, be sure to come with plenty of patience. You are about to discover the true meaning of "red tape." Bureaucratic assholes are amazingly inventive in finding new excuses for delaying the completion of paperwork. And, of course, if your proposal involves even the slightest variation from standard protocol, you will quickly be trapped in an endless loop called "covering your ass." The person you are dealing with will have to consult his or her supervisor, since independent thinking is strictly forbidden in bureaucratic agencies. He will have to consult his superior, and soon your paperwork will be buried and forgotten in a pyramidal pile of postponed priorities.

Nothing makes a bureaucratic asshole happier than to upset a client to the point of complaining. The client, of course, assumes that it is his right to complain. What he does not understand is that the asshole bureaucrat has been well trained in the jujitsu of verbal defense, and is supported by the vast network of the bureaucracy itself, whose first rule of behavior is: "Protect your own."

The asshole clerk will begin by affecting that wonderfully snotty tone of voice used to convey superiority. He will then start quoting regulations and protocol, inventing any rules he needs along the way. If the client continues to argue, the asshole clerk then firmly declares that he does not have to take any more of this rudeness, and walks away.

What the client never knows is that it was time for the asshole's coffee break, anyway.

The only problem for most asshole bureaucrats is that the work day ends after eight hours, and they have to go home to their families, who won't put up with this kind of nonsense. However, they also know that it is only sixteen hours before they can return to the office and go back to work, hassling and intimidating the rest of us.

ACTIVITY

1. Have you ever applied for a building permit? How many assholes had to give permission? How long did it take? How many bribes were involved?

2. Some experts feel the only way to curtail the growth of bureaucracies is to take the fun out of them. Some radical ideas include: that clerks be judged on the number of people they actually help; that all paperwork be limited to one side of a letter-sized sheet of paper; and that all governmental agencies be turned into private enterprises. How would *you* take the assholes out of bureaucracy?

106

12
The "Helpless" Asshole

> There's nothing you can't get your
> family to do, if you're willing to
> swallow an occasional can of Drano
> and get your stomach pumped.
> —Kitty, a recovering asshole

"Helpless" assholes are probably the least loved of all kinds of assholes. They are like dandruff clinging to a black suit—if you brush them off, they are back again in a few minutes.

At first, these people may not seem like assholes; in fact, they seem just the opposite—weak, powerless, and unable to stand on their own. They constantly need someone else to lean on, tell them what to do, and do their work for them. But this is just an act—an image as phony as a three dollar bill. These people are actually quite strong and forceful. They have simply discovered the enormous strength which lies in weakness.

Lucretia Poupulopolis, the well-known family counselor, documents "The Asshole-Centered Family" in *The Greek Journal of Family Therapy*. She reports that the most seriously dysfunctional families were those dominated by the weak, parasitic asshole. "These assholes often tyrannize their entire family—and circle of friends—with their constant need for attention and their incessant effort to control others through intimidating demands for help. They force others to put their lives in holding patterns in order to take care of them. This results in what I call, 'the waiting for Mother to die' syndrome. Of course, dying is the last thing Mother intends to do."

The power in weakness can be awesome. Many assholes know how to drain the last kilowatt out of any situation. If they don't get enough attention, they accuse others of insensitivity to their needs. If they don't receive the help they want, they will turn on the guilt. If they don't get their way, they will feign whatever level of illness will force others to cancel their plans and tend to them.

As one tired housewife complained about her mother, who had moved in six months earlier, "She can whine about a thousand different things in a hundred different ways, but it all means the same thing. She's determined to call the shots."

Indeed, sickness is a great source of power for many of these people. Aches, pains, and indigestion magically appear on cue when needed. One begins to suspect that good health is a distinct threat to many of these people.

The helpless asshole uses many of the standard tools of assholism—whining, guilt, intimidation, and fear—plus a few others. The most notable "extra" tool is what might be called "crazy making."

"Crazy making" is the art of driving other people crazy. It is done subtly and persistently, by making irrational demands, changing one's mind frequently, whining incessantly, and constantly criticizing everyone else. A helpless asshole will tell you that you have never done enough for them and have never loved them enough. He will chastise you for not spending enough time with him, and then tell you to get out of his sight. As Desmond Dickeyton puts it in his book, *Helpless?—Or Just Public Enemy Number One,* "It is enough to drive anyone crazy."

The knack of crazy making includes confusing everyone else with impossible paradoxes. We must never complain about their whining, for example— but we are always expected to respond to it. We are expected to respect their independence, yet take care of their every whim. Because they define the rules, we have no chance of winning at their game.

In family situations, the crazy maker is usually someone who doesn't quite fit—such as a mother-in-law living with the family of one of her children. In business, it tends to be the quiet types working in offices. Every day, they find a way to actually do less and less of the work assigned to them. When confronted, they state a willingness to do the work, but the amount to be done has grown so rapidly it is just impossible for any one human to keep up. If you try to fire them, they suddenly invent lurid stories of sexual harassment or discrimination and threaten to file a lawsuit against the company.

In society, the crazy maker is the professional parasite who protests loudly that he has been denied his rights, while in fact he is busy usurping the rights of everyone around him—in other words, lobbyists and special interest groups.

Like the bureaucratic asshole, helpless assholes are also experts at manipulating time. They can procrastinate so effectively that they make snails look like speed demons. At home, they are always the last ones ready to leave for a family outing. Every visit to the bathroom seems like an eternity to everyone else. They can stretch an hour of housework into a full day's activity. At the office, they routinely keep everyone else waiting. Their greatest skill is their ability to look busy all the time, yet accomplish almost nothing.

The helpless asshole has also learned to play the role of martyr as skillfully as any Oscar-winning actor. These people have learned to speak with such plaintive tones and so many sighs that they always seem exhausted. They can fake fatigue so cleverly that neighbors may start wondering if they *are* being treated as a slave.

As Mrs. Poupulopolis indicates, however, dying is the last thing these people will do. They may occasionally fake a suicide, in order to revive the guilt and attentiveness of people who were starting to become indifferent, but they would always make sure someone would discover them in time.

As one of my patients said after his asshole wife died of an accidental overdose of wrinkle cream, "She was a vampire who took her daily quota of blood in the form of my frustration and guilt. Now she's the devil's problem, thank God."

ACTIVITY

1. Do you have crazy makers in your family? At work? In other situations?

2. Have you ever heard the whine of an asshole? Try to describe it in 100 words or less.

13
The Litigious Asshole

"So sue me," said the elephant.
"I will," said the ant.
"Step on it," said his lawyer.
So the elephant did.
—Old Greek fable.

One of the cherished freedoms of a democratic society is the right to seek justice in a court of law. Under this concept, "the little person" has as much access to justice as a person with money, power, and position.

There is only one fly in the ointment of this theory: assholes. Shakespeare wrote, "The law's an ass." While this may or may not be true, the sad fact is that our legal system heavily rewards assholes.

In this country, any asshole can file a lawsuit against anyone he wants to harass, and force them to spend good money defending themselves. Facts and circumstances are not required—just malice and imagination. And so the courts become an attractive playground for just about any asshole.

The fastest way to lose a lawsuit is to believe that our court system is "fair," unless you are using

111

this term to imply mediocrity. The second fastest way to lose a lawsuit is to hire a lawyer of ethics and integrity (if you could find one). It takes an asshole to fight assholes. Fair has nothing to do with it.

This is because assholes don't care about justice. If they did, they would stay out of the courts. They just want to be able to harass and frustrate their enemies—and their neighbors, co-workers, peers, and local government officials—and do it legally.

It is illegal in this country to slander or libel the reputation of another person. But any asshole who wants to slander you has only to do one thing—file a lawsuit against you in which he lists every slanderous charge he cares to make. If it is slander, he'll lose the lawsuit—but he will have accomplished his goal, all under the protection of the law.

Litigation is an asshole's dream. Assholes love to have someone to blame for every problem, and litigation is the perfect way to let all of society know who they blame for all of their ills and problems, real or imagined. In our modern rush to litigate every possible wrong, assholes have started suing:

• Doctors, for malpractice. If there were justice, the courts would also let doctors sue patients who refused to cooperate with their treatment.

• Corporations, for firing them. If there were justice, the courts would also let the corporations sue their former employees, for defrauding them by cashing their paychecks but not performing their work.

• Teachers, for failing to make them less stupid than they are. If there were justice, the courts would also let the teachers sue their students, for goofing off in classes and wasting their time.

• Their parents, presumably for not having had an abortion.

Sometimes litigious assholes are just petty, such as the lawyer who sued his condo association because his neighbors didn't keep their dogs from pooping on his lawn. Justice slept, and apparently forgot that shit and assholes go together.

At other times, filing suit brings out the full rage and malice of the asshole. This is especially evident in divorce and child custody cases. There is apparently no known limit of taste and reason that an asshole won't exceed in order to get what he or she wants in one of these domestic disputes. Does the court step in and keep these indiscretions under control? Of course not. It is the right of the little person to be as big an asshole as anyone else, and the court vigilantly defends this right.

In dealing with the law, it is important to remember always that lawyers are a high risk group of assholes. It is therefore advisable never to trust a lawyer. If you take his advice, and then it does not work out, your lawyer will deny all responsibility for misleading you. And never rely on the fairness of the opposing lawyer. Lawyers are not paid to be fair. They are paid to protect their client's interests, by ruining yours.

Of course, lawsuits are not the only way the litigious asshole does his dirty work. Many laws and regulations can be enforced through local and state agencies. One well-researched complaint from an asshole neighbor may force you to move the fence you put up last year or the driveway you poured twenty years ago four inches to the right or the left, so that it will comply with zoning regulations.

113

Recently, activist assholes have found the law to be an invaluable weapon. A local neighborhood can probably delay the city from routing a freeway through its heart for fifteen to twenty years—all at the expense of the taxpayers and the inconvenience of those who need the freeway. Conservation groups can now successfully bring billion-dollar-projects to a grinding halt, because they might endanger a snail.

The litigious asshole is never satisfied. The sky is never blue enough nor is water wet enough for his demanding tastes. Since these problems offend him, someone must be responsible—probably you!

One victim of a litigious asshole, sued 14 times in two years, put it this way: "Hell hath no fury like an asshole with an attorney."

ACTIVITY

1. Have you ever been sued by an asshole? Was justice served? Or did the asshole win?

2. Have you ever served on a jury? How many of the other jurors were assholes? How many slept through the trial? How many of them could actually understand English?

3. If you are mathematically inclined, calculate the odds that a litigious asshole would be able to recover from assholism. Warning: you will need to be familiar with imaginary numbers to make this calculation.

Part Three:
When Society
Becomes an Asshole

SIGNS OF ASSHOLISM IN SOCIETY

1. The NRA.
2. MTV.
3. The ACLU.
4. The use of acronyms.
5. Not knowing what an acronym is.
6. Existentialism.
7. *The One Minute Manager.*
8. Book burnings.
9. The size of the federal government.
10. The belief that it's healthy to be angry.
11. High school grads who can't read diplomas.
12. The popularity of *Friday the 13th.*
13. The ability of the military to blow up the world 20 times over. Isn't once enough?
14. Recreational drugs.
15. Televangelism.
16. $19 million governmental studies of the impact of farting cows on global warming.
17. The popular belief that all truth is relative.
18. The Shopping Channel.
19. Actors being paid $1 million for one TV ad.
20. That anyone with only one pair of legs might need 500 pairs of shoes.
21. Co-dependency.
22. Synthesized voices in airports & elevators.
23. LBOs, poison pills, & golden parachutes.
24. The Stealth bomber.
25. Flagburning as an act of free speech.
26. Government subsidies of tobacco farmers.
27. The fact that more people shoplift Preparation-H than any other item.

14
Business as an Asshole

> "We're not making much of a profit,
> but we sure as hell are making a
> new generation of assholes."
> —from *The Butt of Society*

To understand the disease of assholism completely, it is necessary to realize that it does not just attack individuals. Whole groups of people, from businesses to unions, from religious denominations to schools and colleges, can be infected and start behaving like assholes. In fact, the whole of society is often addicted to asshole ways of acting. What is war, after all, other than a massive attack of assholism?

When assholism occurs on this large of a scale, it is referred to clinically as *massholism*—the addiction of large masses of people to asshole behavior. Until now, whenever society has become an asshole, it has just been dismissed as an aberration. Now, we know better. It is an epidemic of assholism.

There are many ways in which society has become an asshole. In the 50's, the McCarthy hearings epitomized asshole behavior. In the 60's, the college protest movement mooned the rest of society. In the 70's, the country as a whole suffered from what Jimmy Carter eventually called a "malaise." But since few people like being called an asshole, Carter was dumped on his ass. The 80's became a decade of "holier than thou" posturing, as politicians, lobbyists, and other assholes tried to create a new agenda to bitch about. Who knows what the 90's will bring? Only one thing is certain: More assholes.

One of the key areas of society which regularly demonstrates asshole traits is business. This is, after all, one half of the dynamic duo, the military-industrial complex, that Eisenhower warned us about many years ago. Or maybe it is more than one half. Since the military has so few wars to busy itself with, it seems to have its hands in the pockets of business as much as business has its hands in the pockets of the military.

The one thing that keeps business from going completely asshole (unlike government), is that the free market generally forces businesses to be productive. Productivity, of course, is alien to the basic consciousness of the asshole. But there are plenty of aspects of business that can shelter both the individual asshole and assholism as a social disease:
- Greed.
- Competition.
- Power grabbing.
- Social irresponsibility.

Take the lust for power, for example. It has driven CEO's of many major corporations into frenzies of buy-outs that have left their own companies

118

crippled with debt. They are then ripe to be bought out by still a bigger fish in the pond. Yet none of this bloodthirsty raiding has shown any signs of improving commerce in America.

The pursuit of excellence is a good thing. But business sometimes forgets its primary purpose—to do its business in an orderly manner. When power games—nitpicking, jockeying for better perks, designing golden parachutes, and gambling on short term results—become more important than serving the public, then business has become an asshole.

• When presidents of companies that post a loss for the year nonetheless receive bonuses of more than half a million dollars, business has become an asshole.

• When businesses stop identifying themselves with the products they make or services they perform, and become nothing but holding companies, business has become an asshole.

• When businesses try to convince us that oil spills pose no threat to the environment, and that sea otters actually like the black goo, then business has become an asshole—in fact, a flaming asshole.

Assholism in business is nothing new, of course. But modern business has managed to refine this arcane art in two significant ways. They have added employee relations and public relations staffs.

Employee relations was invented by business so that it could be an asshole in the way it treats its employees. This department is mandated to find the cheapest way possible to convince employees that the company cares about them. People who manage these departments are carefully trained in

119

all of the usual asshole arts: double talk, cheating, scheming, lying, and intimidation.

Public relations was invented so that business could be an asshole in the way it deals with the rest of the world. The increasing emphasis on PR has raised situational ethics to new heights, making the Watergate cover-up look like a comedy of idiots. In her biography, *Lies, Damn Lies, and Public Relations,* Hermione Honeycutt reveals that her whole success did not jell until she learned to lie with sincerity. "After that, everything else was easy," she writes. "I convinced people that cigarette smoking was actually good for their health. I told people that drunks don't kill people, cars do. I was even successful in convincing people that a little toxic waste in their backyard helped control the weeds and kill off the rats." True to her profession, she denied, just before she died of lung cancer, that smoking had anything to do with her illness. "It was just all that wonderful fresh air in Los Angeles."

The assholism of business is perhaps best codified by Peter Thomas in his new book, *Secrets of Instant and Temporary Success.* In it, he decribes the "trickle down" affect of massholism as it filters through the corporate ladder. He advises:

1. Learn to bullshit creatively.

2. Always cover your ass.

3. Never explain. And don't write memos, lest they be discovered later on. (Avoid tape recordings, too.)

4. Deny everything—except praise.

5. Learn to exploit the talent and hard work of everyone working for you.

6. Always keep an eye on the enemy—govern-

ment regulators, environmentalists, and bank loan officers. They are the real competition.

7. Never kick ass too hard. The asshole you wipe out today may be the chief of the EPA tomorrow.

If this advice doesn't give you instant success in business, never fear—massholism lays an excellent foundation for morassholism.

ACTIVITY

1. If you were asked to sell your grandmother to get ahead in business, what price would you be willing to settle for?

2. If you had the opportunity to stab a competitor in the back, what weapon would you choose to use? What if it were not a competitor, but a colleague?

15
Morassholism

The government *is* the bureaucracy;
the bureaucracy *is* the government.
—Joe Budweiser, spokesperson for
the union of federal employees.

In any nation, government attracts a high number of assholes. The reason why is simple. The government has a great deal of power in shaping the way we lead our lives. Assholes lust for power—in particular, the power to tell other people what to do, how to do it, and when to do it. So they go into government.

There are two major divisions in government. First, there are the politicians—our elected officials. These are the people who think they run the government. Second, there is the entrenched bureaucracy. These are the people who actually do run the government.

Both groups attract assholes—and have fallen victim to becoming assholes themselves. We may be reluctant, of course, to admit that our senators, congressmen, and state legislators are assholes, especially since we were the ones who voted them into office. But in most elections, there is no real choice. It is a question of determining which candidate is the least offensive asshole.

Has our elected government become part of the asshole conspiracy? Let's look at the record:

• Congress has set up automatic pay raises for itself that go into effect every so often unless the members of both houses vote specifically to cancel them. What assholes!

• Congress refused to approve a constitutional amendment forcing them to pass a balanced budget each year on the grounds that it was a gimmick. It should know, since Congress itself has now become a gimmick. What assholes!

• Congress routinely exempts its own members from many of the laws affecting everybody else in the country, including social security. It is as though they view themselves as a different breed of people—assholes!

Although Congress believes that it embodies the power of the people, everyone knows that the real power of government is vested in the bureaucracy— that large group of hundreds of thousands of employees who work for the Civil Service and control our lives. Congress can pass any law it wants—it doesn't matter, because the bureaucrats will interpret and implement the law to suit their own fancy—and survival.

Nowhere is this more obvious than in the Internal Revenue Service. One simple constitutional amendment, passed in 1913, gave Congress the seemingly innocent power to "lay and collect" taxes on the income of the general public. Out of this bland phrase, skillfully written to lull the public into a mood of trust and compliance, the bureaucracy has created the asshole's greatest triumph: the IRS, a blend of Gestapo, KGB, and the Iranian secret police. In a collective fit of egomania, the IRS has usurped virtually every freedom America was founded on, from the freedom to privacy to the freedom to pursue happiness without governmental interference. In recent years, in fact, it is rumored that the IRS has programmed its computer to look for taxpayers who are unusually happy and content with their lives. These are automatically pulled for audits.

So long as the IRS continues to exist and operate under its current commission, there will be rampant assholism in government. But this is not to say that the IRS is the only segment of bureaucracy tainted by assholism. It is clear that bureaucracy has become an asshole when:

• Agencies continue to exist long after the need for them has passed.

• Commissions are routinely formed to study problems that have already been assigned to oblivion by the bureaucratic powers-to-be.

• There is a perverse relationship between increasing the power of a government agency and a continuing decline in the quality of life the agency was meant to improve. Ever since the Department of Education became a cabinet level post, for instance, the quality of education in this country has steadily declined. Rational people would conclude that it is therefore time to disband the Department of Education, lest we end up with total illiteracy. But the assholes are in control!

Why are government agencies so inefficient, and

more apt to make society's problems worse than better? It's because government has become stuck in the morass of gross incompetence, wasted time, and never-ending miles of red tape. It's not just assholism—it's *morass*sholism! In his autobiography, *Confessions of a Department Head,* Gomer Phyle reports, "My department would take longer to process a piece of paper than my compost heap." As one of his critics added, "It always stunk more, too."

There are several ways morassholism clogs up the gears of government. Some of the more notable methods are:

- Meeting mania. Bureaucrats are always in meetings. When any problem arises, it must be studied by committees, analyzed by consultants, reported on by commissions, discussed by review boards, and approved by executive committees. In this way, the actual responsibility for making a decision is completely blurred. Everyone's ass is covered.
- Paperwork. All governmental procedures are carefully regulated by paperwork, to be filled out in triplicate. It takes paperwork even to requisition paper to do more paperwork. If the government's supply of paper suddenly dried up, government as we know it would come to a halt. There would be gnashing of teeth among assholes, but the rest of us would celebrate in the streets.
- Rules. Without rules, bureaucracies would not know what to do, because there is no natural work done by these agencies. Their work is defined solely by rules. Rules also protect the agencies from the public, by restricting the right of the taxpayer to question the obvious fact that the agency is doing

nothing but restrict his freedom. Finally, rules give power to supervisors, so they can more properly tyrannize their subordinates.

The military is perhaps the best example of this facet of morassholism. There is no natural reason to respect or obey a person who is making his or her life's career out of being a drill sergeant. So there have to be rules to justify this anomaly. This is why the military—and the government, by extension— has rules. To justify having assholes in charge.

The most frightening aspect of morassholism is the innate tendency of bureaucracies to expand, like a fat person in a candy shop. Marshall McDroolin, in his book *A Conspiracy of Assholes,* writes: "The only way to hide inefficiency is to grow larger. If something simple doesn't work, make it more complex. It still won't work, but it will be harder for people to figure it out—and far too expensive to change at this point. So the mantra of all bureaucrats is: 'Complicate, complicate, complicate.' "

Is it too late to stop morassholism? If we leave things as they are at present, the grim answer must be yes. Bureaucracies are like the proverbial nine-headed Medusa. If you slice off one head, two more will replace it!

The only hope, therefore, is to commit society as a whole to wiping out assholism, first individual by individual, and then group by group. Eradicating morassholism has never been done before, but then, no one had ever been to the moon before 1969.

Should we leave it to the assholes? Or should we demand an end, once and for all, to all this bureau-crap?

ACTIVITY

1. Has your congressman or Senator ever attended a meeting for recovering assholes? Openly, or in disguise? Do you think he or she ought to be attending these meetings?

2. Would you be willing to participate in a modern day version of the Boston Tea Party by dumping all of the government's paperwork in the Potomac? Do you realize that the Boston Tea Party could not be held today—unless its organizers filed an environmental impact statement far enough in advance that hearings could be held and the necessary permits issued?

16
Religion as an Asshole

> I give to you a new commandment:
> Love one another!
> —Jesus

If an oil company sold bad fuel that befouled our neighborhoods, damaged our car engines, and failed to heat our homes, it would be put out of business. Customers would be outraged. Senators would investigate and demand that the company be fined. The news media would vilify them. Politicians would win election just by campaigning against such a company.

And yet, when the same thing happens in religion, there is barely a whisper of protest or concern. The basic message of most religions, as quoted above, is to love one another—and God. But in most of the popular brands being distributed today, this basic product is being tainted by a lot of bad gas—hateful and harmful ideas which befoul mass consciousness, damage our self-confidence, fill us with guilt and shame, impede creativity, and divide us from each other. Bad religion doesn't even keep us warm—in other words, comfort us in a time of loss.

Why is it then, that good people keep on lining up to be offended, insulted, defiled, and sabotaged by bad religion? And why isn't anyone doing anything to warn them of this danger?

The reason why is simple. Religion, like the government, has become an asshole.

This painful conclusion is reached with the utmost respect and love for God. It is not God who is the asshole, after all—just the many religious zealots who claim to represent His divine love but turn it into a mockery through their teachings and violence.

What are the signs that bad religion has supplanted good religion? There are many:

• When a church makes a big stink over birth control, it is clear that it is spending too much time worrying about plumbing problems and not enough time working for the Second Coming.

• When a major figure in a world religion puts out a death contract on a published writer, it is clear that his faith in Allah can be shaken by a little bad publicity.

• When churches presume to rewrite Scriptures, even though they acknowledge them as the word of God, because they may be offensive to the warped minds of a few people, what does this say about the strength and nobility of our religious traditions?

• When a religion presumes itself to be chosen above all others, but never asks itself—*chosen for what?*—does it still have the humility to be able to guide its people spiritually?

The problem is that these asshole characteristics inevitably rub off on our thinking about God, at least to some degree. As Dr. Alan Stinkfish, founder of the Divine Anti-Defamation Association (DADA) has written: "God never got such a bad reputation until modern times. The Greek and Roman gods, for instance, were swingers, and often interceded to help us poor humans. And the ancient Hindu gods actually thought sex was okay. Modern religion is not only taking all the fun out of life, but is adding to our burdens. Something ought to be done about it."

Dr. Stinkfish cites as evidence the writings of the Ayatollah Jewmania. In his seminal book, *Demagoguery Throughout the Ages,* the ayatollah writes, "Demagoguery was invented, perfected, and institutionalized by organized religion. No one has practiced it down the ages with greater diligence or success. And we intend to keep it that way!"

"The classic problem of religion," Dr. Stinkfish laments, "has always been to help its followers discern the wolves from the sheep. The problem today, however, is that the wolves have found it far more profitable to imitate the shepherd!"

In short, the assholes have taken over, and religion has become an asshole. The churches, temples, and mosques have kicked God out, and opened their doors to the hustlers, the money changers, the rabble rousers, and the quick fix experts.

A surprising number of those convicted for the part they played in Watergate, for example, began new careers in the ministry. What does this tell us about the church today? That it is even less ethical than government?

Just who—or what—is being worshipped during those Thursday evening Bingo sessions?

In whose pocket does all that money sent into the televangelists end up? What constructive good has come from all of this giving?

The church is no longer just a self-supporting neighborhood congregation, drawn together in worship. It is big business, and as such, it has become a takeover target for mega-assholes. It gives them the perfect insider position to fleece the flock.

But it is not the money lost that is the real concern. It's the damage done to our understanding of God. In the hands of these assholes, the holy trinity has been redefined. God the Father is now the real Godfather, who runs Sicily and everything else, except what the Devil controls—which is most people and all real estate south of the pole star. The Holy Spirit has become the ghostly equivalent of the CIA and the FBI, searching for evil everywhere. And the Son of God has been recreated to resemble a wimpy magazine salesman peddling stories of sacrifice and faith.

The damage done has been catastrophic. One of my more perceptive colleagues says: "These religious wrecks are filling up all of my consulting time. They think they are victims of dysfunctional parents, but the more I dig into their cases, the more I find they are actually products of dysfunctional religions. By itself, human nature is not all that bad. These neurotics had to be *taught* to let go of their common sense and fill themselves with this kind of guilt, self-loathing, fear, and irrational beliefs. It could only have come from one source: bad religion."

Is it really bad religion? Or just the signs that religion itself has become an asshole?

ACTIVITY

1. Is there such a thing as a lost soul, or are we hearing too much from religious leaders who just ought to get lost?

2. Did our Creator create meanness in people, or have mean people created mean stories about God?

3. Did religion teach you:
   - To be a decent human being.
   - To be an asshole.
   - To feel guilty about being an asshole.
   - All of the above.

17
Reading, Writing & Assholism

> "Would you read my high school diploma to me?"
> —a recent graduate to his mother.

A researcher investigating the decline in education asked a graduating senior why he thought ignorance and apathy were so widespread among modern graduates.

"I don't know, and I don't care!" was the senior's reply.

A more accurate answer came from a senior who did not qualify for graduation: "Aw, the schools are all run by a bunch of assholes."

Actually, there are many fine, dedicated people in the teaching ranks. But the bureaucrats in charge of telling teachers how and what to teach are a different story. At this level, assholism prevails. And as the balance of power for schools has shifted from the local school board to state and federal bureaucracies, our educational system has become an asshole.

The indicators are plentiful:

• When more than half a school system's students drop out when they reach age 16, our schools have become an asshole.

• When high schools graduate students who cannot read or write, our schools have become an asshole.

• When colleges must add remedial classes to teach freshmen what they were supposed to learn in grade school, our schools have become an asshole.

• When teachers can be fired because they paddled a misbehaving child, and yet the same child can beat up a teacher without serious consequences, our schools have become an asshole.

• When students are denied the right to pray in school, each in his or her own way, then our schools have become an asshole.

• When school boards must spend more time on forced busing and other social programs than on the quality of education, our whole society has become an asshole.

Being assholes, those who are responsible for this decline are adept at avoiding the blame. The teachers' union insists that teachers are blameless; local school boards claim they are powerless; and the state and federal governments will issue a report on the subject when they are done studying it twenty years from now. As one critic says: "Schools are more skilled at analyzing the problem than at looking for solutions. In fact, they don't seem to know the difference."

So, we are told that the deterioration of education is due to everything from acid rain and the lack of vitamins to the rising incidence of poverty and crime. Even worse, many people are encouraging us to accept educational incompetence as the norm. One educational psychologist, Dr. Jerome Cuphead, tells us not to worry. "If modern graduates cannot read, they can still get the information they need from radio, TV, and tapes. If they can't add, they can use a calculator. And if they don't know where they are, they can stop and ask a policeman."

Sure—and get arrested for loitering. Society expects certain minimal skills from its adults. Lowering our standards will not solve anything. We have to face the truth, as bitter as it may be. Our educational system has become an asshole.

How did this happen? Who was asleep on the watch and let this occur?

Hermann Eichman, who spent five years studying this problem, concludes that the underlying cause is an increasing fear of being accused of discriminating against stupidity. In his monumental book, *Why Johnny Can't Read and Doesn't Give a Damn,* Eichman writes: "Everyone has become afraid to hurt the student's feelings by flunking him. So they have dumbed down the textbooks, watered down the tests, and generally pander to the lowest common denominator. If this is not enough, and a child still fails, why, they pass the dumb-dumb anyway!"

Others blame the rising influence of child psychologists in the academic setting—people who have preached that a permissive atmosphere is essential, lest the creativity, spontaneity, and feelings of the student be repressed. High self-esteem and good social skills have assumed greater importance than learning to think.

Educators are beginning to see that this was a mistake. In a riveting article in *The Journal of Juvenile Education,* Molly Goldbud writes: "The only thing the lack of discipline or lowered standards does is spoil the student. Yes, we have high self-esteem now—students actually feel good about being stupid. Yes, we have creativity—students have become very creative in making excuses for being absent or not doing their homework. Yes, we have spontaneity—students are always interrupting classes by screaming and getting into fights. Yes, we have made sure that no student is ever traumatized by the need to repress his feelings. As a result, they behave like assholes pretty much all the time. Some of them even expect police protection while they peddle drugs in the school yard."

Our schools are failing to serve the needs of our students. As a result, they are failing to serve the needs of society. It would be wrong to assume, however, that they have not been serving any purpose at all. The school system does work. But for the last thirty years, it has been held hostage to do the work of certain special interest groups who wanted to use the universal school system to make sweeping changes in society.

Let's face it: anyone who would deny a generation of children the right to a good education, just to promote his or her own pet cause, is a flaming asshole.

The only way we can improve the quality of education is to kick the assholes out and let education return to its primary purpose: teaching children to think, read, and write.

It's a tall order, but I think it can be done. The

first step, in my opinion, would be to introduce a new course in the high school—and maybe even the college—curriculum. It would be Social Studies 901—How To Spot An Asshole. Necessary supplies for this class would be 1) a copy of *Asshole No More;* 2) a flashlight, for looking in dark places; 3) a mirror, for obvious reasons; 4) names and addresses of the school board and administration; and 5) a list of all the books banned at the school library. These books will be mandatory reading.

The final exam for this course will consist of explaining why these books were banned—and what you learned by reading them.

ACTIVITY

1. List ten primary mental skills you use every day. How many of these did you learn in school? How many did you learn outside of school?

2. What percentage of what you learned in school has been of direct use to you since you graduated?

18
Assholism in the Media: The True Epidemic

The most entertaining fiction I read
is in the newspaper every morning.
—Oliver South

And then there is the media—newspapers, television news crews, magazines, radio stations, and wire services. I have saved them for last because, if there is any one segment in which assholism has reached epidemic proportions, it is the media.

In fact, the media is a perfect model of the complete asshole:

• It is arrogant. It loves to refer to itself as the "fourth estate," as though it were equal in power and importance to government and religion. In this country, it wraps itself in freedom of the press, as a justification for any and all anti-social behavior—but spends little time examining or promoting the responsibilities that go with this freedom. As one pundit who prefers anonymity has put it, "Freedom of the press and assholism just don't mix."

The press also arrogantly believes itself to be the sole custodian of truth in this country, even though it wouldn't know truth if it were mugged by it. It seems to subscribe to the old notion that if a tree falls in a forest, and no one is there to hear it, there is no noise. As this applies to the media, reporters seem to believe that unless they cover an event, it never happened—unless, of course, a competing paper or station covers it, and then they all get their asses chewed out.

This concept in reverse then becomes their justification for being allowed to participate in every drug raid, city council meeting, board meeting, or invasion of another country that arises. They have come to believe that only they can prevent scandals, mischief, and wrongdoing.

• It lusts for power. Since it can't have real power, other than the power to destroy people's reputations, it must settle for second best—to be envious of the power other people have. This often leads to a preoccupation with the abuse of power, which can become so obsessive that the media ends up looking for a scandal in every politician's bedroom and every business executive's boardroom.

To satisfy this lust for power, the media is preoccupied with reporting about important people—people who seem to have power. If a person of high position catches a cold, it will be front page news. But if he passes it on to seventy-five of his subordinates, it's treated as a non-event.

Most of all, the media loves to invent news. Reporters and broadcasters get tired of always having to stick to the facts; they yearn for creativity. So, they go out and find a group of bums and incite them to riot. Or, they just make up quotes as necessary and attribute them to unnamed sources. In

139

this way, they satisfy their primal need for power.

• The media is shallow. No story is so complex it cannot be reduced to a ten-second sound bite, or a three hundred-word article. And yet the media never feels obliged to mention that there are shades of grey to the story they just reported in black and white hues. They see themselves as an innocent Dorothy in the land of Oz, surrounded by wicked witches who must be attacked, fraudulent wizards who must be exposed, cowardly lions who must be condemned, ignorant scarecrows who must be ridiculed, and heartless tin men who must be vilified.

• It is rude. Reporters delight in finding the angst and struggle in every story. They are trained at an early age to barge in on grieving widows and ask them how they feel about their husband being killed after falling from the tenth floor of a building under construction. Yet when the widow answers truthfully, "Like kicking you in the balls, you asshole," they never include it in the story. They just make up something suitable instead.

• They believe their opinions are more important than the facts. If anyone questions the validity of this charge, just read *Time* for a year.

The media makes a pretense of being fair, but still end up looking like the assholes they are. They love to interview some big-mouthed radical, and then leave most of the radical's bizarre statements unchallenged. After being repeated a number of times, people start to embrace these ridiculous statements as though everyone agreed on them.

Yet when the media interviews someone they despise—for example, a well-known government official—they will try to skewer him or her with the most vicious questions imaginable. Anyone who dares protest this glaring inconsistency is immediately labeled an enemy of free press and blackballed by the media.

• They try to control public thought. Instead of reporting the facts about a story, one of the favorite tricks of the media is to ask people who know nothing at all about the subject to give their opinions on it. Then they print or air those opinions which most closely promote their own point of view.

• They are innately destructive. The media lives to destroy public officials and figures. Sometimes, it is a reporter or anchor working all alone who manages to ruin a mighty figure; at other times, it requires a conspiracy among several key newsmen, who will decide that they have been too nice to so-and-so, and now is the time to "rough him up." It is then only a matter of time before the individual in question will be discredited, embarrassed, and forced to resign in disgrace.

When, years later, the person manages to clear his name at last, the story will not even be picked up by the wire services.

• The media, of course, will deny these charges, but then denial is one of the prime characteristics of assholism. From time to time, the media will respond to public charges of bias, but their response is limited to broadcasting a forum stacked with professional news people. They will talk about the charges in a serious tone for twenty-five minutes or so, until—right on cue—a senior member of the press speaks up and intones once again the blanket protection of "freedom of the press." Everyone quickly asserts his or her agreement, and the assholism of the press is covered up once more.

We therefore cannot rely on the media to expose this epidemic or cure it. They are the disease! To halt it, we must learn to think for ourselves and demand that the media behave more responsibly.

When George Bush was elected president, one prominent newspaper snidely instituted "The Quayle Watch," to report the presumed peccadillos of the new vice-president. What we need to do is tear a page out of the media's own manual, and institute "The Asshole Watch," a daily examination of the abuse of responsibility by national and local media—newspapers, TV news, radio, and magazines.

Of course, finding a newspaper with the courage to print it may be a greater miracle than the raising of Lazarus from the dead.

ACTIVITY

1. Write a letter to the editor, accusing him of illicit love affairs, the acceptance of bribes, and any other scandalous charges you can think up. Tell him your charges are documented by unnamed but reliable sources. His response will let you judge just how free the free press actually is.

2. Practice exercising control over the media. Everytime you hear TV or radio newspeople act like assholes, turn off the set and read a good book.

Part IV:
Living With Assholes

19
Working with Assholes

Oh, shit. Another asshole.
—George, on meeting his new boss

Unless you are independently wealthy, retired, or unemployed, you probably have to work with assholes. And yet, very few people know how to get along with assholes. We are not given training on this highly important subject. It is just assumed that we can figure it out on our own.

Of course, many people question if it is possible to work with assholes and retain even an ounce of self-respect. It's not easy, but I am happy to report that it can be done.

The place to begin, however, is with yourself. To cope successfully with assholes, you must be well motivated and well disciplined. You must ask yourself a series of tough questions:

• How much do I like my job?
• How much do I need my paycheck?
• Is this job worth the agony of putting up with this asshole?

You will be tempted just to chuck it all and go elsewhere. This is not the point of this review.

Remember, even if you do get another job as good as this one, you will probably have to work with assholes there, too. The purpose of this review is to build up your determination to cope with the assholes around you.

The next step is to review your options. There are several:

• You can choose to *compete* with the assholes you work with. This is not recommended, because it means you will have to become an asshole, too. But you will be an inexperienced asshole, and that will put you at the mercy of all these much more accomplished assholes, who are already expert at lying, cheating, intimidating, passing the blame, and evading responsibility. If you try to beat them at their own game, they will chew you up and spit you out. So don't even think about it.

• You can attempt to *reform* the assholes. As a therapist who has worked with thousands of assholes, let me assure you that it is impossible to reform an unrepentant, uncooperative asshole. Even if the asshole is pledged to recovery, it is a very difficult task. So leave the work of reforming assholes to professional therapists. Don't add to the swelling number of burned out, hollow-eyed wrecks of decent people who have been destroyed by their heroic but misguided efforts to reform an asshole.

• You can learn to *survive* with assholes, which is to say, surviving with your humanity, self-respect, humor, and dignity intact. This will require all of your charm, skill, and cunning! But if you can learn to do it, you will be at work long after the assholes have departed.

The first rule of working with assholes is to remember that appearances mean everything to them. A *show* of interest, cooperation, affection, respect, or even fear is generally enough to satisfy them and make them think you are wonderful. But it must be a sincere display of affection and respect. Assholes have practiced phoniness all of their life; they are experts at spotting fake phoniness.

Second, strive for clear communications. The asshole expects to be noticed, greeted, listened to, agreed with, complimented, reassured, and congratulated. Go out of your way to say things like:

"Thank you."

"You're right."

"Gee, that's so clever of you."

"I'm sorry."

Just don't expect them to ever say any of these things to you. Communicating with an asshole is a one-way street.

The third step in planning your strategy for coping with an asshole is to define his or her relationship to you. Is this person your boss, a subordinate, or a colleague? Each must be handled differently.

• Handling an asshole boss. Assholes are very insecure about their authority, so they are very sensitive to real or imagined threats to it. Never do anything that threatens your boss's authority! Instead, learn to treat him as though he were a minor deity or visiting royalty. Be enthusiastic in showing an interest in his goals and programs. Greet him each day as effusively as possible. There's no need to go overboard—like keeping a photograph of him on your desk and burning incense in front of it—but a discreet bow or curtsy now and then may help. Try to use "sir" or "ma'am" whenever possible, but don't embarrass your boss by using phrases *in public* such as "your lordship" or "your ladyship."

With this show of loyalty, your boss will think you are wonderful and give you special treatment— like getting to go home before 8 p.m. on ordinary work days and getting to eat lunch two or three times a week. At the Christmas party, you may even be allowed to serve the hors d'ouevres and drinks.

• Handling asshole subordinates. The treatment is just the reverse. You need to treat them as little, petulant, sensitive, frightened children in adult bodies. Restrain your urge to shout at them or strangle them from time to time. This will only frighten them and hinder the process of bonding.

Subordinate assholes frequently whine about their work load. Remind them that you had to do these same things when you were in their shoes; someday, they, too, will have an assistant to take care of these duties. Until then, it's tough luck. If they persist in whining, remove their coffee and copy privileges until they stop.

They may also try to sabotage you by not getting the work done. Take them aside for a long talk and tell them how the entire office is depending on them. This should appeal to their ego. If it doesn't, then punish them by making them arrive fifteen minutes early each day to make the coffee and recommending that their Christmas bonus be a lump of coal.

Then, when you hear of the first opening in a department run by an asshole colleague, recommend your unrepentant subordinate to fill the position. In this way, you can deal with two assholes at once.

- Dealing with asshole colleagues. These pose the most difficulty. To treat them as a minor deity would be the same as giving them permission to be an asshole. To treat them as a child would only provoke them. Like any asshole, these people will try to act like your boss but behave like a little child that needs spanking. Resist that temptation!

Instead, treat them as you would an unwanted guest at home—say, your mother-in-law. You must be diplomatic in dealing with them, and yet take a stand at the same time.

This calls for all your charm and skill. You must define boundaries and decide how to share responsibilities with this asshole. It also requires a certain understanding of assholism.

In meetings, for instance, you can win points with asshole colleagues by supporting them at the proper moments. This is generally early in a project, before they have had a chance to generate any specific ideas. Make a statement like: "Based on Joe's past track record, I support this idea of his completely. Can you give us a clearer picture, though, of how it's going to unfold?" Joe, of course, will not be able to do this, because he stole the idea from someone else. But he will be so happy to have your support that he won't notice the hidden innuendo of your question.

The hardest problems to deal with are his inevitable invasions of your turf. What do you do when he steals some of your accounts from you, or suggests to your boss that you might be using drugs? The worst thing to do is to pretend that it didn't happen. Instead, confront your colleague and congratulate him on his marvelous sense of humor.

Tell him that it is so wonderful to find a colleague who enjoys playing practical jokes. Ask him to be sure to let you know how much he enjoys the little pleasantries you have prepared for him. Also ask him whether he prefers the smell of horseshit or cow manure. Then do nothing. His own worries about what you are planning will attract major disasters, without you having to lift a finger.

Of course, it is not possible to be comprehensive in these suggestions. For more hints and ideas for working with assholes, be sure to read *Canoeing in the Workaday Cesspool, How To Swim with the Barracudas and Float with the Turds,* and *Bullet-Proofing Your Self-Respect Without Losing It.*

ACTIVITY

1. Who are the assholes you work with? How well are you coping with them at present?

2. Practice smiling at them while they are being rude and obnoxious. If this is too much of a strain, practice first with only their photograph. Resist the temptation to throw darts at it, however.

3. Mentally rehearse handling their put downs and insults with politeness and courtesy. If they like to make fun of the way you dress, for example, rehearse saying, "Thank you for pointing this out to me. It will help me dress for success."

4. Keep reminding yourself how much you enjoy receiving your paycheck.

5. Also remind yourself that you only have to deal with this asshole eight hours a day. He has to live with himself twenty-four hours a day. Now, that's a real curse!

20

When A Friend is an Asshole

Do you believe in telepathy? I do. I
have one asshole friend who frequently calls me to unload all of her
unhappiness on me. I always know
when she's going to call me. For a
full minute before the phone rings,
I fart uncontrollably.
—Alice, a friend to many assholes

No one wants to believe that a friend of theirs
may be an asshole, but it does occur in this imper-
fect world of ours. Sometimes they become infected
by assholism long after we have befriended them.
In other cases, they are situational assholes, and it
was a long time before a situation arose that brought
out the asshole in them. Or they may have been
such an accomplished sissy asshole that we never
suspected that they weren't really sincere.

Before learning how to live with asshole friends,
therefore, we need to establish some basis for decid-
ing if and when our own friends have become assholes. Each of the following would be a strong hint
that your friend is an asshole:

• You are expected to remember at all times that it is a privilege to have them as a friend—a privilege you must earn over again each week.

• They do not reveal any of the rules of this friendship until it serves their interest. They assume a real friend would never doubt their motives.

• They can change these rules at their convenience. You, however, can't.

• They reserve the right to call upon you at any time for any kind of assistance they deem necessary—to get a loan, to babysit their kids, to provide an ironclad alibi, or to borrow your house. If you are a true friend, you must never question their right to do this—or ask any favors of them.

• They have the right to dump all their problems on you, and expect you to be endlessly sympathetic and attentive. No matter what the problem is, you are expected to side with them and reassure them that they are completely in the right. If you have a problem, on the other hand, you are expected to keep it to yourself, so that it will not drag them down emotionally during this time of stress.

• You must hate all of their enemies. They will be insulted if you try to be friends with anyone they hate or have discarded.

• You must shower them with endless praise, affection, support, and encouragement. Anything less than wild enthusiasm will be viewed as tepid.

• You must never criticize them for anything. Any discussion of mistakes they may have made would injure their self-esteem, so it must be overlooked.

If, after applying these criteria, you are still

unsure about certain friends, observe how your cat or dog behaves in their presence. If they try to cover them up with dirt or kitty litter, take this as a strong indication.

Once you have determined that a friend is an asshole, there are several steps to take immediately. These include:

1. Realize that with a friend like this, not only do you not need enemies, apparently you can live without friends, too. Get real! Tell them that the only reason you let them hang out with you is that you are: a) doing penance for an old murder, or b) collecting material for a book you are writing on severely neurotic people.

2. Remember that genuine friends don't make rules about friendship, but they do set sensible limits and boundaries. Borrowing your car for a month, for instance, is unacceptable, unless they pay you rates comparable to Hertz or Avis and bring it back with a tank full of gas.

3. Tell them that if they insist on using you as a psychotherapist, you will expect them to schedule appointments in advance and pay you $100 an hour for your time.

4. Inform them that their enemies have in fact used good judgment and dignity in dropping them from their "A" and "B" lists. In fact, if you didn't keep a "C" list, they would be history for you, also.

5. Tell them that you have started keeping track of the many times they bitch and whine, and that soon you should be able to submit your files to the *Guinness Book of World Records* for the endurance record in putting up with continuous bitching and petulance from a friend.

6. Move, and leave no forwarding address.

Of course, how well each of these suggestions works will depend upon the nature of each individual asshole. Also keep in mind that some of these suggestions may provoke violent responses such as screaming, vile accusations about your parentage, and a sudden shower of unidentified flying objects aimed directly at you.

If this occurs, just stand back and look hurt. Tell your friend you will not talk to him or her again until an apology is offered.

With luck, he or she will be too much an asshole to do it.

ACTIVITY
1. Do you have friends who are assholes?
2. Why?

21
Married to an Asshole

> I knew the romance had gone out of
> our marriage when he no longer
> removed the cigarette from his
> mouth before he kissed me.
> —Mary Jean, married to an asshole

There may be no greater shock in this life than
to wake up one day and realize you are married to
an asshole. Some people learn the sad truth within
moments of saying their wedding vows; others do
not discover it until years later. How long it takes
to discover it—if it is true—is not terribly important, however. What is important is understanding what it means to live with a spouse who is an
asshole.

The kinds of tactics that allow you to survive
working with an asshole or being a friend of one just
will not work with a spouse. What are your options? Not many. The primary ones include:

• Divorce. This is not recommended, because
there is only one thing worse than being married to
an asshole, and that is being divorced from one. If
you survive the court proceedings and the financial

ruin, your ex-spouse will then spend the rest of your life making sure you live to regret what you have done. And because your ex-beloved is an asshole, the chances are extremely high you will.

• Assume an alias and escape to a foreign country. This has merit, but is probably unworkable, for all of the reasons cited under divorce—unless you can cleverly fake your death before leaving the country.

• A discreet suicide. More drastic than option number two, but probably preferable to option number one. It's major drawback is that it is irreversible.

• A discreet homicide. As an ethical therapist, I cannot advocate either this option or the previous one. Nonetheless, there are situations where this one might be worth considering. If you ever need help, I have a good friend Guido...

• Learning to live with the asshole. Let's face it. This is your only serious option. And it is not by any means impossible, if you just keep a few tips in mind:

1. Accept the fact that you are not going to cash in on the American Dream. Better luck next time. The sooner you can lower your expectations about your marriage, the better. This will also help you avoid being too depressed whenever you remember that it was you, and only you, who chose this spouse.

2. If you are still depressed anyway, lower your expectations even further. Get to the point where you are *glad* you married an asshole. Think of all the good things that can come out of this arrangement. For example, since your spouse is an asshole,

this gives you an object lesson to point to when you tell your kids not to be assholes themselves.

3. Learn not to be bothered by verbal abuse, long sullen silences, total neglect of your feelings, and the absence of affectionate support. It is not necessary to become an alcoholic to achieve the desired state of emotional numbness—just learn not to care. Once you have cut yourself off in this way, you'll find the pain disappears rather quickly.

4. Check out discreet alternatives. Seek friends of the opposite sex who are also married to assholes. This gives you something in common, and you can probably compensate for whatever it may be that you're not getting at home. If you cannot fill the gap in this way, my friend Guido is also professionally associated with many fine services that can provide just what you want.

5. Be as affectionate and agreeable as possible with your spouse. This will cut down considerably on the friction and hurt you experience. When arriving home from work, for example, let your first words to your spouse be: "I'm sorry. Whatever it is you're unhappy about, I'm sorry." This kind of blanket confession will tend to take the wind out of his or her sails, and spare you much discomfort.

6. If your spouse will not tolerate an easy win, but insists that you fight back, then you have not just married an asshole—you've married a flaming asshole. The solution to this type of situation is to help your spouse find ways to drain off excess rage and anger. Encourage your spouse to take adult education classes in guerrilla warfare, hand grenade tossing, and hand-to-hand combat. Be sure to take up karate yourself.

Will marriage counseling help? You bet it will. As Colonel Sanders, professor of military strategy and marriage counseling at West Point, states it is important for such couples to participate directly in marriage counseling—not as patients, of course, but as bad examples. Through both direct presentations and home video highlights of their greatest arguments, asshole couples can help ordinary people understand that they don't have it so bad after all. By comparing their marriage to that of the assholes, they can see that they have a foundation of common interest and love to build on, and so their marriage is worth saving.

Many people accuse Sanders of being a cynic, but not because of his stand on this issue. It is due to his firm belief that bad marriages cannot be cured—they can only be prevented.

His ultimate advice, when the urge to marry becomes strong, is: "Just say no."

ACTIVITY

1. How many bad marriages can you count among the people you know? Were they incompatible—or just assholes?

2. How many bad marriages have you had? Why do you keep on getting married?

22

The Born Asshole

I knew it was going to be a bad day
when he strangled the cat before
breakfast.
—Joan, mother of a 4-year-old
asshole

For generations, child psychologists have assumed that there is no such thing as a rotten kid—just innocent victims of bad parents or disadvantaged social conditions. Every time a child behaved like a genuine brat, hordes of therapists would step forward immediately to heap blame on the parents and society.

My own research indicates that some obvious and relevant facts have been ignored.

Everyone knows that you can plant carrots or petunias yet end up with more weeds than vegetables or flowers. The same can happen in raising children. Some kids turn out bad despite having a healthy home environment and decent parents. In fact, some kids are just born mean and destructive.

• They delight in torturing insects and other small animals.

- They beat up on kids younger than themselves.
- They sass back to their parents.
- They measure a good day in terms of property damage.
- They refuse to eat their vegetables.

In short, they are born assholes—asshole children of decent parents.

Dr. Montague Fishburger, professor of child psychology at the University of Milpitas, claims that psychologists have become addicted to their theories of child abuse. As a result, they are always blaming the parents and presuming the child to be innocent.

"This is not true," Dr. Fishburger states flatly. "I have three kids and they are all flaming assholes. My wife and I have given them a stable, loving home environment with fair and consistent supervision and lots of affection. We encouraged all of the right behavior; we were supportive, forgiving, and friendly. We urged them to be independent and creative, and to take on greater responsibility. Yet they all turned out rotten."

How rotten? They all got together and decided to nail their elementary school teachers—two women and a man—by accusing them of sexual abuse. They created several lurid stories and carefully memorized them, so that they would not contradict each other when questioned separately. Then they told their parents, who naturally got quite upset, and immediately complained to the principal. The three teachers were fired and charges were filed against them. They were eventually cleared, when it turned out that one of the stories had been lifted verbatim from a short story published in *Playboy*. But the teachers had suffered two year's of humiliation, court costs, and loss of pay by that time. And Dr. Fishburger was professionally embarrassed by having been conned by his own children.

Were their jeans too tight—or were they born assholes? Mrs. Cassandra Tightgut, the founder of the controversial but effective "Tough Luck" movement for difficult children, certainly concurs with Dr. Fishburger.

"The week I turned thirty-six, my sixteen-year-old daughter had her second abortion and my fifteen year old son was arrested for selling drugs. I decided to get revenge by having my tubes tied, even though I knew it was only a symbolic gesture.

"While I was in the hospital, I thought about all the times these brats had abused our kindness and helpfulness. I realized that my husband and I had perhaps been too helpful. It was at that moment that I conceived of the 'Tough Luck' approach to raising kids. I began to lecture on the program, and parents everywhere went wild. They swarmed to hear me. There are now twelve thousand 'Tough Luck' support groups throughout the nation.

Tough Luck is a no-nonsense way that decent parents can handle asshole kids. It is based on the following principles:

1. It is not your fault that your kids are rotten, unless you actually spoiled them. Nor is it your responsibility to make life comfortable for them. All you need to do is be fair, as your own adult common sense defines fair, and then be tough about being fair. If your sixteen-year-old complains about

not being able to use the car over the weekend, remind him that Abraham Lincoln walked nine miles to school each day, *each way*—and they named a car after him. When your kid says, "Yeah, a car for old farts," you should serenely reply, "Tough luck!"

2. If your kids are crying and whining, check them for broken bones and open wounds. If none is found, tell them to shut up and stop blubbering. Whatever has upset them, it's just their tough luck.

3. If your kids get out of line and start being uncooperative or irresponsible, cut them off. Tell them they should leave home now while they still know everything. If they don't like the way you are running things at home, tough luck! (Children under three are exempt from this rule.)

4. When you find your children playing with matches and homemade Molotov cocktails, and then sneer at you and say they are going to burn the house down, call the police. A few nights in jail should do wonders for encouraging appreciation for the true comforts of home. If they complain about their treatment in jail, tell them, "Tough luck!"

5. Tell all of your children who are six or older that they must do their share of the housework or else pay rent. It is never too early to begin training in the work ethic and wholesome self-discipline. If they rebel, tell them it's tough luck.

6. Ban all music composed after 1960. Do not let them watch MTV, or any television other than PBS. If they protest, shoot the TV set and tell them it's tough luck.

7. Impose strict limits on homework. If they fail once a week to get it done, knock off TV privileges.

If they get careless and let it slide to twice a week, force them to spend the night listening to Wayne Newton albums. When they complain, say: "Tough luck."

8. When your kids rebel, do not hesitate to spank them. If they are older, whipping may be more effective. Some parents shudder at the thought of corporal punishment. But think about it. If your kid is behaving like a little asshole, can there be a better way to communicate with him than by beating him on the butt? If he cries and say it hurts, just tell him, "Tough luck!"

9. Ban all locks on bedroom doors. Carry out search and destroy missions in your kids' rooms daily. If drugs, weapons, condoms, or other contraband are found, confiscate them and feed your kids only bread and water for two days. If they protest, tell them, "Tough luck."

This program will do one of two things. It will either inspire your asshole kids to make a complete turnabout and become decent children again, or it will drive them to run away. In either event, you are the winner.

No more asshole children!

ACTIVITY

1. At what age do you think children reach maturity and can fend for themselves? 21? 18? 12? As soon as they start talking back?

2. Have you spanked your kids today?

23
Adult Children
Of Asshole Parents

> I never knew my first name wasn't
> "Hey Asshole" until my kinder-
> garten teacher called me "Kevin."
> —Kevin, an adult child of asshole
> parents

Historically, perhaps the most neglected group of people victimized by assholes were their children. Kids who were physically abused have been able to get help for some time, but until recently, children who suffered severe emotional abuse were left to their own devices, which meant they grew up thinking they were crazy—or at least guilty of some horrible sin. Now they are learning that they are just adult children of asshole parents. They are still crippled when it comes to acting in the adult world, but fortunately there is a growing number of books, workshops, support groups, and specially trained therapists eager to help them recover from their asshole parents.

This is of great importance, because studies

have shown that children of asshole parents have a strong tendency to become asshole parents themselves, unless they learn otherwise as adults.

There is no magical cure for twenty years of exposure to assholes during the most formative years of our lives. But these people can now at least draw immense comfort from knowing that they are not responsible for their wretched lives. As one victim of asshole parents put it, "My therapy is proceeding a lot faster now that I know whom to blame. And I feel so much better now that I hate my parents instead of myself."

The majority of adult children of asshole parents (ACOASSPs) are highly motivated to overcome the curse of their childhood treatment. This is evident as soon as they become adults, even before they enter therapy. There are certain signs that are dead giveaways:

• At the first chance, they move as far away from their parents as they can. Most of the state of Alaska, in fact, is populated with ACOASSPs.

• They deliberately ignore their parents' birthdays. It's not that they want to ignore these occasions—it's just that Hallmark has not yet come out with a "Thanks for Nothing" line of greeting cards.

• They go through a fantasy period in which they deny that anyone in the world could possibly be an asshole. This is a time of great vulnerability to them, as they become high risk candidates to marry an asshole and repeat the whole cycle over again. It is therefore important for these young adults to get professional help!

What are the real problems behind the hate, despair, self-rejection, fear, and sense of inadequacy experienced by the ACOASSP? Years of research indicate that they can be summarized as follows:

1. Difficulty in bonding with human beings. Harry, a recovering ACOASSP, says, "I never knew that there were people who were not obnoxious, corrupt, and devious until I was 23 years old. I guess I kept seeing a bit of the parental asshole in everyone."

2. Difficulty in bonding with themselves. Having been surrounded in their early years entirely by assholes, ACOASSPs tend to assume that they are just as bad as their asshole parents. Virginia, an ACOASSP in her third year of therapy, now enjoys being herself and liking it. "When I was a child, I wanted to grow up and be an asshole just like mother. But now I see how much that's harmed me! I want to be me! I'll do it my way! Does anybody know my name?"

3. Difficulty in thinking. ACOASSPs were not allowed to think or have their own opinions as children. Consequently, they tend to procrastinate, have a hard time making decisions, and may openly rebel against established rules. Their fear of committing some unpardonable error or being condemned for independent thinking has inhibited their minds. Alice, another recovering ACOASSP, is proud of her liberation from the tyranny of her parents. She has formed a chapter of the Flat Earth Society in her adopted town of Paducah, Kentucky, and is beginning a campaign to save the duckbilled platypus.

4. Difficulty speaking. The words of many ACOASSPs were often shoved down their throats

as children. As a result, they have a fear of expressing themselves as adults. But with effective therapy, the average ACOASSP can learn to express himself or herself more eloquently than the standard range of "Yes," "I'm sorry," and "Please, don't hit me again." In the more successful cases, they even learn how to yell and scream, and are now able to place orders at the drive through at Wendy's. Others talk back regularly to their car radio and love it.

5. Difficulty laughing. Some ACOASSPs were brought up in such sober and grim circumstances that they thought laughing was only for overt schizophrenics and the very, very nervous. Therapists have now developed a three-month crash course for these unique victims, which consists of watching old movies of the Three Stooges and Charlie Chaplin for twelve hours a day. Over 95 per cent of those who complete this program are able to laugh spontaneously and openly thereafter—especially if they see someone wearing a derby hat or sporting a cane.

6. Difficulty shitting. This may strike some people as odd, but ACOASSPs have spent so much of their life holding in their feelings that many of them end up holding *everything* in. Laxatives prove ineffective in these cases. What they need is toilet retraining. Some therapists, though, have reported good results by hypnotically regressing ACOASSPs to the time of their toilet training and teaching them that it's okay to shit for themselves, not for their parents. Thereafter, they are able to flush with confidence.

7. Difficulty relaxing. ACOASSPs are often

very tense from years of having to keep up their guard against criticism and abuse. Once they learn that the enemy is no longer their parents, but their own fear of being yelled at, they can relax. In some of the more successful instances of recovery, they have been able to revisit their parents and snore right through a long boring lecture about how much they've changed, and aren't Momma and Poppa's little darling baby any more.

8. Fear of wire coat hangers. This is frequently accompanied by an unwillingness to say, "Mommie Dearest." With the advent of plastic coat hangers, this problem is slowly disappearing.

One of the great problems of dealing with ACOASSPs is precisely the fact that they are adults, and as such, often believe they have taken care of their problem. They no longer live with their parents and see as little of them as possible. But this is exactly why these people need therapy. Having failed to resolve these conflicts in a meaningful way (by spending thousands of dollars in therapy), they will continue to look for the mother or father they never had in all of their adult relationships—in the person they marry, the friends they associate with, and so on. As a result, these relationships will not be very healthy ones, until the parental issue is resolved.

For this reason, I recommend ACOASSPs to take the following steps, in or out of therapy:

• Make peace with your asshole parents. Go visit them and tell them you are ready to bury the hatchet. Tell them you now understand how difficult it was for them to treat you well as a child, and that all is forgiven. If you want to be kept in the will,

168

avoid mentioning that you now realize that they are assholes.

• Review all of the attitudes you absorbed from your parents. Throw out any that border on assholism and replace them with noble humanistic qualities. If, for instance, upon arriving home from work, you get angry at your dog for mixing your martini too dry, you are being over controlling and intimidating, just like your parents. Apologize to your dog—unlike humans, he will probably forgive you—and tell him you won't bark at him again.

• Forget your parents. It only takes one flush. (If it doesn't, you'd better call Roto Rooter.)

If you are dealing with parents who have died, visit their graves. In this case, you don't have to worry about calling them assholes—it's too late to be cut out of their will. In fact, you can show your resolve to overcome their influence by telling them you're going use part of your inheritance to make a major donation to the Society for Sterilizing Assholes (that's ASS backwards).

Vast strides are being made in the diagnosis and treatment of ACOASSPs. If you are one yourself, you may want to check out your local support group and attend some of their workshops. For additional reading, I recommend Chris Awford's impressive book, *Daddy Deadliest*.

ACTIVITY

1. Were you a victim of asshole parents? How do you know?

2. How has this affected your life as an adult?

3. When do you plan to grow up?

Part V:
The Road To Recovery

24
Stages of Recovery

> After you eliminate all the bullshit, only the bull is left.
> —Ben, a recovering asshole

The hardest step on the road to recovery from being an asshole is always the first one—*the recognition that you are an asshole.* No one wants to admit that he or she is an asshole, and so this is an extremely painful moment—a moment that requires great courage and determination.

Often, the moment of recognition is precipitated by some major crisis, thereby compounding the intensity of the pain. The asshole goes through bankruptcy, a divorce, being fired, a terminal illness, the death of a loved one, or, worst of all, being wiped out by an even more powerful asshole.

Wounded and humiliated by Life itself, the asshole's defenses are severely weakened. The usual tricks of rationalizations, excuses, blaming others, screaming, lying, and whining are no longer enough to bail the asshole out. It's the truth that hits the fan, instead of their usual line of bullshit. In the depths of despair and confusion, the asshole finally comes head to head with himself. He is an asshole!

If this is a true moment of recognition, the asshole will have a sense of liberation, almost exhilaration. Unfortunately, it is a moment that cannot be forced, something that family members, colleagues, and friends will often attempt to do. They will confront the asshole with his or her behavior and say point blank: "You are an asshole." But unless the asshole is ready to hear this, the charge will fall on deaf ears. The asshole will say, "The hell I am!"

This is what is known clinically as *denial,* and it is the most common barrier to recovery not just for assholes, but for anyone suffering from addictions. Even though their behavior is as evident to everyone around them as the zit on the end of their nose, assholes will refuse to see the truth. True to form, they will hide behind rationalizations:

"I'm just a social asshole."

"I'm no more an asshole than you are."

"What you see is what you get."

"It takes one to know one."

"I don't need therapy. I can work this out on my own."

"If you love me, what does it matter to you?"

Even after the magic moment of true recognition, denial is still a threat to the recovering asshole. He or she must take action right away, lest the old traits of rationalization and blaming others revive. The asshole must get to know himself—he must *discover the core issues* behind his many years of assholism.

What does this mean? The asshole must actually confront his own bullshit—his basic emptiness of values, lack of caring, lack of responsibility, and lack of honesty. He must also admit his tendencies to be lazy, to intimidate others, and to win by cheating or lying. Only by recognizing and admitting ownership of these core issues can the asshole break the vicious cycle of blame, self-pity, and despair.

This attempt to plumb the depths of his assholism will require many lonely and agonizing hours. The asshole must learn to stand in front of the mirror of his mind and cry out, "Why did I do this to me—the person I love the most? How could I be so cruel? How could I be so stupid? Why? Why?"

In my own case, I had to realize that all those years of medical training and helping others as a proctologist had not given me any special privileges. It is not what you know that makes you an asshole; it is how you act. And some of the biggest assholes of all are those in the so-called helping professions. I am the proof of it.

I had to disregard this outer shell of achievement and probe until I found the emptiness within me. This, I realized, was the core of my assholism— the hole that had to become whole. When I first tapped into it, I felt as though I was falling through a black hole, a bottomless abyss. Only later did I realize that I had fallen into it years before; now I was actually climbing out of it.

Clinically, this experience is what is known as "bottoming out." You realize how completely your whole life has been sucked into this hole.

One of my patients—a lawyer—described the same phenomenon a little bit differently. "The

175

moment I finally got in touch with my emptiness, it felt as though I were in an earthquake. I knew intuitively that I—and all lawyers—were fakes, frauds, con men. I saw myself as P.T. Barnum, lining up the suckers. Justice was no longer a blindfolded woman, but an old hag playing craps."

If the recovering asshole can endure this brutally honest and thorough self-examination, the next step in recovery—*the contrition phase*—can then begin. Impelled by a genuine desire to make amends, the recovering asshole actually begins to dismantle the rotten habits he has accumulated: arrogance, pettiness, meanness, dishonesty, fault-finding, anger, and cynicism.

This effort will typically seem to leave the poor asshole weak and defenseless. His world is being turned upside-down. Former strengths that he habitually relied on and trusted—arrogance, lying, and manipulation—have turned out to be junk. His impenetrable ego of steel is now riddled with rust. Worst of all, his long-imprisoned conscience is now beginning to resurrect itself. He feels guilt, doubt, and even sympathy. It's a terrible time for the recovering asshole, for he's on the brink of actually becoming human! It's a time of terror and hesitation. Unless there is competent support from friends and professional therapists, the whole process of recovery can be aborted at this time.

The example of one of my patients illustrates this nicely. Melanie was in her twenties and was a recovering asshole bitch. She had been dating a nice fellow for several months, and was well on her way to rebuilding her life. At her weekly group therapy session, she asked if she should go to bed with him. One of the newer members of the group made the unfortunate comment, "What have you been doing with him all this time? Learning multiplication tables?" The sarcasm ripped her apart, and she realized that she had not actually dealt with her bitchiness—she had just chosen to inhibit it instead of express it. This was too much for her. She broke off her relationship and, on the rebound, found a real slimeball she could bitch at and nag to her heart's content.

Melanie lacked the contrition she needed to recover. Her asshole past proved to be too strong, and overwhelmed her efforts to grow up.

However, with courage, wisdom, luck, and the help of God and friends, the asshole can plug the hole in his or her self-respect. He or she is then ready to move onto the fourth phase of recovery— sometimes called *the regenesis phase*. This is the delicate process of building up decent human qualities, most of which will be totally unknown to the recovering asshole. In this phase, he must learn to:

- cooperate with others.
- share authority.
- delight in the achievements of others.
- accept blame for his or her own mistakes.
- trust others.
- let others think for themselves.
- express compassion.

The recovering asshole must learn that it is okay to fail sometimes—or even to be ignored. He learns that it is all right to let others have authority, and that it is fun to do things without an ulterior motive or strategy.

He must also learn to deal with other assholes

from an entirely new perspective. This may cause some friction, because as he learns what assholism really is, he may well discover that some of the friends and colleagues who told him he was an asshole just a few months ago need to be told the same thing—by him!

There is no end to this final stage of recovery, for the recovering asshole must never forget that he was an asshole once—and can become one again, if he drops his guard. He cannot rely on Life or others always to treat him fairly, so he must build up his own internal resolve to become a decent human being (DHB) and stay that way.

This is the goal of recovery: to become a DHB. It is not to become a saint or even a perfect person— just an ordinary, likeable person who consistently acts in a decent, intelligent way, no matter what life deals him.

As Sally, a recovering asshole, put it: "I feel great. I'm not running around with my head up my ass any more."

ACTIVITY

1. How long did you deny reality before you recognized that you were an asshole?

2. How many DHB's do you know? What are their common characteristics?

25
Tools for Recovery

I'm an asshole, but that's okay:
I'm getting nicer day by day.
I'm in recovery, to learn to do good
And treat other people as I should.
—Recovery song

Drug addicts, alcoholics, and chain smokers all have been known to go "cold turkey"—they have broken off their addiction suddenly and completely. It is not possible to do this, however, as a recovering asshole. It is not just a change in behavior that redeems the asshole—more importantly, it is a change in character.

The work of recovery is more than a question of courage, hard work, and luck. The asshole has to be purged, reprogrammed, and redirected. Arrogance must give way to humility. Rudeness must give way to courtesy. Meanness must give way to compassion. Anger must give way to helpfulness. None of this can be accomplished unless the asshole cultivates the necessary tools of recovery—the humanistic skills which will let him redeem his character and become a DHB.

There are five basic tools the asshole can use.

179

Each of them plays its part in the work of recovery—of turning the asshole inside out, so that he or she becomes human once again. Let's look at each of the five.

Group Therapy

Group therapy should be the cornerstone of psychotherapy for the recovering asshole. In the early stages of recovery, the asshole is still more ass than whole. He is prone to relapsing into his normal state of arrogance, rudeness, and meanness. Group therapy helps keep him honest. It reminds him that he absolutely must give up his asshole ways. He can't just go on bluffing and bullshitting, because there are bigger and better assholes surrounding him, and they won't let him get away with his usual tricks.

There's another factor as well. As he looks around the group he is sharing therapy with, he will think to himself, "Boy, I don't want to be like any of these losers!" Then he will realize that he *is* one of these losers. He's an asshole! This should strengthen his resolve to reform.

Individual Therapy

Individual therapy can usually proceed along normal lines, as long as the therapist is specially trained in treating dishonest, intimidating people who tend to deny that they have any problems at all. On occasion, however, it may be necessary to develop new techniques to deal with special cases. If the asshole has pent up a tremendous amount of anger and rage, for example, it may be worthwhile to hold therapy sessions at a bomb demolition site.

Shock Therapy

Some assholes will resist ordinary therapy. For them, it is necessary to devise special programs, designed to shock them back into a sense of decency. This is not electroshock therapy, of course; it is what we call "psychoshock therapy." Here are some examples.

• If you are dealing with an unregenerate asshole who refuses to admit it, send him to work for the meanest asshole in town. This will restore his sense of balance, and give him valuable lessons in humility, patience, self-control, and accountability.

• For the typical "helpless" asshole, shock therapy might consist of just getting a job—preferably on an assembly line or cleaning offices at night. This gives relief to the family members who have been putting up with the asshole's demands, and forces the asshole to become assertive and self-reliant.

• A more drastic example of shock therapy is to have the patient enter a monastery or convent for six months and take vows of silence and chastity. This will give him the chance to explore the depths of his shallowness, without risk of drowning.

• Force the asshole to watch at least ten hours each day of videotapes of himself throwing temper tantrums, or until he breaks down and confesses that he *is* mean and obnoxious.

• Enroll the asshole into a boot camp for mega-assholes, where he will be taught the relationship between promises and deeds, loyalty and friendship, and the boot and the asshole.

Should these measures fail, you must be dealing

with an unregenerate asshole. He is not ready to recover from his assholism, and no one is going to be able to help him. So, there is only one thing left to do—arrange for him to go into a line of work where being an asshole is a virtue and an advantage—televangelism, the law, or tax collection.

Assholes Non-Anonymous Leagues

Once the asshole has entered into the second phase of recovery, the discovery of core issues, it is helpful to encourage him to join a support group of other recovering assholes. These groups are called Assholes Non-Anonymous Leagues, or ANAL, for short. These are similar to Alcoholics Anonymous, except for one key difference. They are nonanonymous instead of anonymous. It reveals the great uniqueness of assholism as opposed to other addictions. Alcoholics and over-eaters need to be able to stay anonymous, and for good reason. But assholes have hidden behind a shield of their slyness and deceit for far too long. They need to be exposed to the full force of guilt and shame. This does not happen in an anonymous setting!

For this reason, all ANAL members are required to run a signed announcement in the local paper confessing their addiction to assholism. One typical form of the announcement is as follows:

"I am an asshole. I am truly sorry for the harm I have caused, and I humbly ask for your help in repairing the damage I have done, so that I may become a decent human being."

In Assholes Non-Anonymous, group members learn to confess, in public, their habits of bullying and exploiting other people. They learn to overcome their tendencies to deny responsibility and blame others for their problems. They report on times during the previous week when they have backslid into dishonesty, cheating, and irresponsibility, and discuss ways to avoid these problems in the future.

In short, they provide a safe haven for the recovering asshole—a place where he can let his deepest problems hang out and still be supported.

The steps for forming and operating an ANAL recovery group can be found in *The Manual for Assholes Non-Anonymous,* commonly known as "The Manual." These guidelines spell out the absolute necessity of forbidding two activities during these meetings: whining and blaming. All assholes are addicted to these habits, and unless kept under control, an ANAL meeting could quickly degenerate into nothing but a bitch and blame session. As a result, whenever a recovering asshole happens to lapse into a diatribe of whining or blaming others, it is the duty of everyone else in the group to stand up, point their fingers at the offending member, and chant: "Tough luck! Tough luck!"

Another requirement is that each member must bring to each meeting a story of a selfless act he or she has performed since the last meeting. This is sometimes the most difficult part of recovery. More than one member has been thrown out of ANAL because they made up a fictitious story of self-sacrifice.

When recovering assholes can truthfully claim that they have been clean of all acts of assholism for at least a year, they are given a party and a button to honor the occasion. The button reads: "Wiped Clean and Ready To Roll!"

The Twelve Step Program

The Twelve-Step Program was first developed for recovering alcoholics. It has been adopted by other kinds of addicts as well—drugs, overeating, and gambling. It can be a powerful tool for helping assholes, too—but it must be presented correctly.

In the early days of treating assholes, the Twelve Step Program was presented without instruction to a group of recovering lawyer assholes. Within one month, the whole group had collapsed, because they had spent all of their time arguing over whether this was to be construed as a legal contract, an opinion, or a loose collection of moral aphorisms. Some thought it ought to be expanded to fifteen steps; others thought it was too hard as it was, and wanted it streamlined down to eight.

To eliminate these problems, I will briefly state the Twelve Steps as they apply to assholism.

1. Admit that you are addicted to behaving like an asshole, and have found no power within yourself capable of controlling it. This has made your life and the lives of others a living hell.

2. There is a Higher Power that created men and women to be decent human beings. Somehow, you got created, too.

3. You must stop whining and bitching and turn your will and life over to this Higher Power, in the hope of becoming a decent human being.

4. Make a searching and fearless inventory of yourself—your crimes against humanity as well as the healthy qualities and skills you possess. You may not find much of the latter, but what you do find is all yours.

5. Confess the exact nature of the harm you

have done. This confession can be made to God, your conscience, or a decent human being—whichever one is still willing to listen to you.

6. Pledge yourself ready to be purged of all assholism. Ask the Higher Power to help.

7. Stop making excuses for why you are still an asshole. Act as though you were a decent human being. If necessary, strain!

8. Make a list of everyone you have bullied, lied to, cheated, ignored, or treated like slaves. Pledge yourself willing to make amends to all of them. If applicable, you can substitute the phone directory of the city you live in for this list.

9. Go forth and make amends to the people on this list whenever possible, except when compelled by court order never to see or speak to them again.

10. Monitor your daily behavior. When in error, promptly admit it. If this is too hard, hire a private detective to take pictures of you, and then use them to blackmail yourself.

11. Through prayer, meditation, and groveling, try to improve your contact with the Higher Power—but without presuming to have become a special person gifted with the word of God.

12. Having been awakened, carry this message to other assholes through the way you act and cope with daily life.

This program can be used individually or in conjunction with a trained therapist. The therapist will help you realize just how widespread your selfishness has been.

The value of working with a therapist is most easily seen in connection to step four—taking inventory of your strengths and weaknesses. Most assholes can figure out their weaknesses on their own, but few have the ability to grasp the nature of the humanistic qualities they are supposed to develop. Compassion is a good example. This is a quality the reforming asshole must cultivate. But the average asshole thinks of compassion as something to take advantage of in a wimp. His way of looking at life must therefore be turned inside out.

The step of confessing the harm you have done can also be a bewildering one, if attempted on your own. If you are like most assholes, you have spent years avoiding God, killing your conscience, and driving friends away. It is therefore natural not to know where to turn to re-establish contact with one of these forces, so you can spill your guts.

The work of actually purging your asshole ways and replacing them with something better is a long and complex procedure. To make it more easily attainable, it may help to think of this process of purging as though it were a fast—total abstention from food, so that your physical system is cleansed. In this case, however, you want to fast from being an asshole—in other words, refrain from acting in asshole ways. The key to success is to take one asshole habit—say, rudeness—and spend one whole week fasting from it. The second week, choose a different asshole habit—say, vindictiveness—and try fasting from it for seven days.

The goal of recovery is to stop using these asshole habits. In order to do this, you may have to give up some of your old goals—such as winning at any cost, making other people feel uncomfortable, and destroying the reputations of others.

Naturally, lapses are bound to occur—after all,

you're an asshole! Just give yourself a modest shock from an electric wire for each relapse that occurs. Pretty soon, you won't be backsliding at all.

Once the fasting has proven successful, the next step is to try to express the positive counterparts of these rotten habits—for example, to be truthful, cooperative, grateful, friendly, cheerful, and helpful. Once again, the best way to proceed is to choose one of these qualities and work for a solid week on expressing it. But keep in mind that as a recovering asshole, you have a delicate system. Do not overload yourself by straining too hard to be helpful. It may take many repetitions before you have the slightest clue what helpfulness is.

These are the tools you can use in recovering from assholism. None of them is magical; they work only if you make them work. And don't feel selfish about using them. Get into therapy; join an ANAL group. You are an asshole—you've got to go.

Go. Don't sit at home being an asshole. Go. As one of my patients said, "I couldn't bear the thought of exposing myself to a bunch of assholes. But now that I've done it, I can't wait until next week to do it all over again!"

Remember: Only you can wipe out assholism.

ACTIVITY

1. Have you confessed to anyone that you are an asshole? If not, write a memo of confession and post it on the office bulletin board. Don't forget to sign it—with *your* name.

2. Join an ANAL group. If there is no group locally, start one.

Epilogue

> I don't know who I am, but at least
> I know I'm not an asshole anymore.
> —Neil, a recovering asshole.

Throughout history, various kinds of therapy have been used for reforming assholes. In ancient times, assholes were either sold into slavery or sent off to work as a galley slave. Flaming assholes were either beheaded or entombed alive. During the middle ages, they were burned at the stake. (It is an error to assume that everyone burned at the stake was a witch. Some were just flaming assholes who got too close to the straw and burst into spontaneous combustion.)

As humanity evolved, these methods of treatment have become more humane as well. Asshole dipping, in which the asshole was tied to a long pole and dunked in the river, was popular among the Puritans. Slightly later, purging the blood stream with leeches gained great popularity. There was also a short period of time when assholes were simply forced to wear the "scarlet letter," which was "A" for asshole. This practice was later adapted to the punishment of adultery.

These forms of therapy had their benefits, of

course, but they also had some awesome side effects. Fortunately, the development of modern psychology has allowed us to treat the modern asshole with the latest and best practices of psychotherapy.

The challenge to the recovering asshole is still immense, however. It is almost inconceivable for anyone who is not a recovering asshole to appreciate the enormous pain of learning to live again with a conscience, to develop genuine feelings of guilt and remorse, to experience actual empathy for others, and to cultivate humane values.

As assholes recover, they go through a total change of identity, values, and behavior. Many lose most of their friends in the process, and sometimes their jobs, too. Their family becomes confused and uncertain. For a while, no one knows who they are, not even themselves.

It would be hard enough just to deal with this tremendous emotional turmoil, but the recovering asshole must deal with a great deal more as well. He must find the strength to face each day without his usual habits of scheming, lying, and bullying. He has been stripped of his arrogance and rudeness and must work all day long as an equal with everyone around him. He has forgone the simple pleasures of intimidating others with sarcastic jeers, and must strive to be kind and helpful. He can no longer resort to cheap tricks to shift blame onto others. He must stand up and face the music alone. Worst of all, he must now be productive and accountable, instead of lazy and devious. This is a heavy burden, indeed—and one that every one of us should sympathize with.

Quite simply, these people need our support—

189

and understanding. We no longer live in barbaric times, when assholism was thought to be a character flaw. We live in enlightened, liberated times, and know that assholism is a contagious disease. We're all vulnerable to it. We must all help cure it.

The life of the recovering asshole is a constant struggle fraught with the risk of relapse and a continuous feeling of despair and loss. The admitted asshole must now learn to live with doubt and guilt, instead of repressing it, and deal openly and honestly with the complexities and ambiguities of life.

But the recovering asshole also knows the joy of becoming a human being again—and being accepted into the fellowship of DHBs, where trust, cooperation, acceptance, and friendship are honored and treasured, not scorned. This joy compensates the recovering asshole for the pains and hardships of the road to recovery.

I wanted to write this book many years before I actually did. But I was still an asshole then, so I'm glad I didn't. It would not have been the same book. It would not have been a beacon of truth for the assholes of the world. It would have just been a collection of my own personal garbage.

I hope that this is what you've learned by reading this book—the difference between garbage and truth. Sometimes they both come in similar packages, and we don't know which is inside—until we open them. Then, we can usually tell by the stink.

This is true with assholes as well.

Come, let us clean up the stench together.

Asshole No More.

Please?